NINE BEST PRACTICES
THAT MAKE THE DIFFERENCE

In A Nutshell

s e r i e s

The Hungry Brain: The Nutrition/Cognition Connection
Susan Augustine

inFormative Assessment: When It's Not About a Grade
Robin J. Fogarty and Gene M. Kerns

The Adult Learner: Some Things We Know
Robin J. Fogarty and Brian M. Pete

How to Differentiate Learning: Curriculum, Instruction, Assessment
Robin J. Fogarty and Brian M. Pete

A Look at Transfer: Seven Strategies That Work
Robin J. Fogarty and Brian M. Pete

Close the Achievement Gap: Simple Strategies That Work
Brian M. Pete and Robin J. Fogarty

Nine Best Practices That Make the Difference
Brian M. Pete and Robin J. Fogarty

Twelve Brain Principles That Make the Difference
Brian M. Pete and Robin J. Fogarty

Data! Dialogue! Decisions! The Data Difference
Brian M. Pete and Catherine A. Duncan

Cooperative Learning: A Standard for High Achievement
R. Bruce Williams

Higher Order Thinking Skills:
Challenging All Students to Achieve
R. Bruce Williams

Multiple Intelligences for Differentiated Learning
R. Bruce Williams

NINE BEST PRACTICES THAT MAKE THE DIFFERENCE

In A Nutshell
collection

Brian M. Pete • Robin J. Fogarty

Skyhorse Publishing

Library of Congress Cataloging-in-Publication Data is available on file.

Print ISBN: 978-1-63450-352-5
Ebook ISBN: 978-1-5107-0120-5

Printed in China

Contents

Preface

We educators know that what makes the difference in the learning journey of the children in our classrooms is quality teaching. We also know from the research what quality teaching looks and sounds like. Quality educators go where the research on the pedagogy of "best practices" leads them.

Through a meta-analysis of studies on instructional strategies, Marzano, Pickering, and Pollock (2001) have identified nine families of strategies that significantly increase student achievement. The results of this meta-analysis point educators to a proven pedagogy with teacher-tested, tried-and-true techniques that work to increase student achievement through cognitive and cooperative efforts.

Framework for Quality

Nine Best Practices That Make the Difference presents research-based instructional ideas that encompass an essential repertoire for beginning and developing teachers as they become skilled professionals. The skills are organized in a "framework for quality" that includes observable skills in four instructional areas: Creating an Environment for Learning, Teaching the Standards of Learning, Structuring Interactions with Learning, and Reflecting about the Learning.

If caring professionals know what works and what makes the difference in the learning journey of every child, they must not only examine but also embrace these ideas in their K-12 classrooms. If, in fact, these best practices are the *proven practice* of effective instruction, they do, indeed, provide a rich yet manageable mandate for the teaching and learning processes.

Best Practices That Make the Difference

The strategies in the nine families are not unknowns to most teachers. Readers might want to check off in Figure Preface.1 those they have used in the past. The rest of the book examines each family in more detail.

1SD	Finding Similarities and Differences
2SN	Summarizing and Note-taking
3RR	Reinforcing Effort and Providing Recognition
4HP	Homework and Practice
5NR	Nonlinguistic Representations
6CL	Cooperative Learning
7OF	Setting Objectives and Providing Feedback
8GH	Generating and Testing Hypotheses
9QCA	Questions and Cues and Advance Organizers

Figure Preface. 1.

Acknowledgments

No book writes itself. In fact, even though the authors write the *manuscript*, they rely on a skilled team of professionals to transform their thoughts and words into the printed pages of the book others eventually read. Our first acknowledgment must be directed to Bob Marzano, Debra Pickering, and Jane Pollock for their timely and thought-provoking publication, *Classroom Instruction That Works*, that is the basis of this Nutshell book. In this succinct piece, the authors have assembled a memorable and manageable set of instructional strategies that are proven to increase student achievement. They have given the professional teaching community an invaluable resource.

Dedication

To Michael Henry Pete, new teacher extraordinaire

About This Nutshell Book

All Nutshell books, including this one, are designed with the teacher in mind. Nutshell books are meant to be an informal conversation between authors and teachers that briefly visits, or revisits, ideas about teaching and learning. They are intended to spark teachers' thinking as they question the ideas presented with their usual pragmatic query, "How can I use this tomorrow?" The ideas are presented in a user-friendly way that translates educational theory into sound classroom practices.

In this book, each family of strategies begins with a list of its strategies and a visual family icon. These two elements set the stage for the discussion of individual strategies. Although there are nine families of best practices framed by the research, there are actually 20 strategies discussed in detail. Each of the 20 strategies is addressed using three elements: A Story to Tell, Things You Need to Know, and A Tiny Transfer to Try.

Each strategy is introduced by title and is accompanied by the family icon. Then, in the first section, A Story to Tell, a story illustrates the essence of the strategy in folksy, everyday language. Telling a story for each strategy is motivated by this short proverb:

Tell me a fact and I'll learn.
Tell me the truth and I'll believe.
But, tell me a story and it will
live in my heart forever.

In addition, along the margin of the story, we give a list of synonyms for the strategy to help readers pinpoint the concept.

In the second section, Things You Need to Know, two questions—What's It All About? and Why Bother?—help unpack the strategy by defining and describing it, presenting a few examples, and discussing its implications for the K-12 classroom.

Finally, in the third section, A Tiny Transfer to Try, teachers find a practical application that they may use immediately in their classrooms. The Tiny Transfer is meant to solidify the concept and prime a teacher's pump by showing a way to start implementing what has been learned.

We hope these ideas are just the beginning of the conversation. The real discussion continues as knowing teachers move along this practical path of professional investigation. Enjoy!

Family of Strategies: Finding Similarities and Differences (1SD)

Strategies

Comparing and Contrasting

Classifying

Metaphors

Analogies

Comparing and Contrasting

A Story to Tell

"The Mustang has the 'five on the floor' gear box that I want. It's in my price range, and they have it on the lot. On the other hand, the Firebird has the leather interior, the larger trunk space, and I love the color."

"Do I tell the truth, which is gonna get me in big trouble, or do I avoid the conversation and delay the inevitable?"

Synonyms—Comparing and Contrasting

similar and different

alike and different

ying and yang

matching and not matching

same and different

aligned and not aligned

Life is full of decisions—big and little ones. These decisions require careful consideration that often involves comparing and contrasting various elements. Finding similarities and differences is a skill that can be practiced and learned.

Things You Need to Know

What's It All About?

Comparing and contrasting is an analysis skill of finding similarities and differences. You *compare* the attributes that are alike, but *contrast* the ones that are different. Comparing and contrasting is like shopping: both require careful consideration, both involve looking at similarities and differences, and both often result in a final judgment.

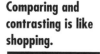

Comparing and contrasting is like shopping.

To analyze by comparing and contrasting is to find how things are the same or different. When comparing and contrasting, two patterns often emerge: the ab-ab pattern and the aaa-bbb pattern.

In comparing and contrasting the two characters of the boy and the man in the novel *The Old Man and the Sea*, the ab-ab pattern calls for comments about one character, followed immediately by parallel comments about the other character. For example, "The boy cared deeply about his old friend. The old man cared as deeply about his young friend." Using the aaa-bbb pattern, there might be a full paragraph about the characteristics of the boy, followed by another paragraph about the various attributes of the old man. For example,

"The boy admires the old man's knowledge of the sea and he listens ever so intently to everything said. The young one wants to learn to be a great fisherman, just like his friend and mentor.

The old man, on the other hand, loves the company of his young friend and enjoys his role as the wise old sage. He knows this youngster has what it takes to become a great fisherman. He tries to show him the ropes as only he knows them."

Why Bother?

Implications for students are numerous. They need to know how to analyze—how to take an idea apart to look at its inner core. In doing analysis exercises, students find similarities and differences as they learn to think critically.

> **[Students] need to know how to analyze.**

A Tiny Transfer to Try

One Stop Shop

Set up participants in pairs. Using the idea of two kinds of shopping (traditional *in-store shopping* and non-traditional *on-line shopping*), practice writing the two narrative patterns of comparing and contrasting: pattern ab-ab and pattern aaa-bbb. Partner A uses the ab-ab pattern to compare and contrast one characteristic at a time, while partner B uses the aaa-bbb pattern first to describe one type of shopping fully, and then to describe the other type. Compare the two patterns: ab-ab with aaa-bbb. Share your paragraphs. Compare and contrast how the two patterns are alike and different. Discuss which might be easier or harder, in your opinion for your students.

Classifying

A Story to Tell

As an illustration of the skill of classifying, the teacher asks her middle schoolers, "How to you arrange the clothes in your closet? Tell a partner." Here are some of the responses she might receive.

"Summer clothes and Winter clothes…Heavy clothes and Light clothes"

"By Color. All the blues together, all the blacks and so on."

"By Long sleeves, short sleeves; long pants, shorts…"

"By Work clothes! Play clothes. Dressy clothes!"

"I have three categories: Fat, Skinny, and In-between!"

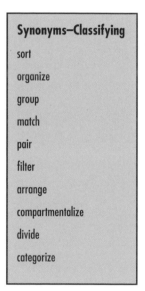

Synonyms–Classifying
sort
organize
group
match
pair
filter
arrange
compartmentalize
divide
categorize

Finally, one young man said, very directly, "I have those that are hanging and those that have fallen on the floor."

The arrangements are not only creative and somewhat humorous but also offer a good illustration of how the brain searches for patterns and tries to organize things into meaningful groups.

Things You Need to Know

What's It All About?

Classifying organizes by sorting according to similarities. Things that have similar attributes are separated from those that don't share those similarities. Classification is like an egg carton: both have compartments that separate and divide, providing a specified place for each thing and a unifying element that brings the individual items into a connected whole.

Gardner (1999) identifies the skill of classifying information as the intelligence of the naturalist. In the sciences, classification skills reign supreme, as students learn about the quintessential, ultimate classification system of mankind: kingdom, phylum, class, order, family, genus, species.

Classification is like an egg carton.

Classifying involves looking for similar attributes in a set of things while discerning the differences between individual members that may place a specific member outside the set. For example, in mathematics, the process of identifying attributes is called set theory. When examining figures, does the large, yellow triangle fit the set that calls for large, red, four-sided figures? Set theory requires the student to match items to strict criteria. A member is either in the set or outside of the set—it's either an example or a non-example of the set.

Typically, everyday "classified" items include: the yellow pages in the phone book, plants in the garden, classified ads in the newspaper, Web site topics on the Internet, products in the grocery store, athletic shoes or candy on store shelves, books in the library; magazines on the racks, CDs in the music world, soft goods in the department store, and even sports teams (territorial divisions). In more official settings, classifying takes on the form of ZIP codes, telephone area codes, shipping zones for courier delivery services, and demographic data about communities, cities, and countries.

Why Bother?

Connections to schooling for the skill of classifying information are infinite. As an organizing skill, classifying helps students manage lots of incoming information. As another analysis skill, classifying is linked directly to critical thinking. For example, in language arts, students encounter overwhelming amounts of input that must be quickly and accurately sorted: words into nouns, pronouns, verbs, or adverbs; sentences into statements, questions, or exclamations; reading material into poetry, biography, mystery, science fiction, historical fiction, or nonfiction.

Students are constantly asked to use their abilities to classify information in order to make sense of the world around them.

In physical education classes, student learning involves a number of classifying activities: separating various muscle groups (large, small; back, abdomen, shoulders, legs, upper body, lower body); recognizing types of sports (field, court, stadium); unscrambling the kinds of equipment (balls, rackets, nets, sticks, paddles); and distinguishing individual sports (golf, skiing, cycling) from team sports (baseball, football, basketball). In short, students are constantly asked to use their abilities to classify information in order to make sense of the world around them.

A Tiny Transfer to Try

Making Sense of Things

Use cooperative groups of 3 to 4 members. Assign roles: recorder, materials manager, reporter, and encourager. Provide large poster paper and markers for each group. Display a random group of words taken from a section of a textbook. Ask the groups to make sense of the displayed words and to write a scenario of the selection. See Figure 1.1

Basketball	Joe's Bar and Grill
Northern Lights	Fence post
Feed lot	Harvest
Cable TV	Seed
Chewing tobacco	Gasoline
Ice box	Apple pie
NRA	Sleigh bells
Cheerleader	Hayrack
4H	Tractor
"Bud"	Corn

Figure 1.1 Classifying words.

Discuss the conclusions each group reached as they critically analyzed and categorized the words. Think about how to use these ideas in reading assignments in content areas.

 # Metaphors

A Story to Tell

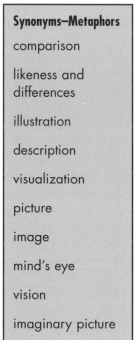

Synonyms—Metaphors
comparison
likeness and differences
illustration
description
visualization
picture
image
mind's eye
vision
imaginary picture

Many years ago, back when the earth was cooling, several participants stopped by after a workshop on Critical and Creative Thinking. As the first woman stepped up to me, she reached out to shake my hand and greeted me with these words, "This was great! I really enjoyed the day, but I can't use these ideas with my kids or my content." Needless to say, I was disappointed in her remarks.

As she turned to leave, another, younger woman plunged toward me and hugged me with all her might. She gushed with compliments about the day and said something I remember vividly to this day, "You have changed my teaching forever. I can never go back to what I was doing before, I know too much now, about how to make my kids think. Thank you for making it so easy for me to take these ideas back to my classroom," and off she went with a bounce in her step and a huge grinning smile on her face.

■□■□■

The contrast between the two participants was so striking, it took me a minute to recover. And I remember thinking to myself, "What is it I did for the second woman that I did *not* do for the first woman? Why can one see *no* relevant possibilities, while the other one sees myriad ways to use the material we had worked with today? What might I do differently to foster transfer for all the participants?"

Later, as I tried to describe to my colleague the incident of the woman who didn't see any relevant connections from the workshop to what she was doing in the classroom, the image of an ostrich with his head in the sand came to mind. The metaphor suggested to me that, in this case, the learner had her "head in the sand" (intentionally or not) and was missing the obvious connections that others could see.

The metaphor of the bird implies certain traits about the learner and her ability to transfer ideas, just as the use of the metaphor of the brain as a computer implies that the brain is similar to a computer. Of course, every metaphor has its limitations, so, although some things are similar between a brain and a computer, there are some things that are different.

Things You Need to Know

What's It All About?

A metaphor says an object is another object, which is not literally the same but suggests similar attributes for the two objects.

■□■□■

Eisner (1979) uses the metaphor of a "connoisseur" to fully describe the complexities of expertise needed in the classroom. His choice of metaphor hints that the astute subtleties possessed by, for example, the connoisseur of fine wines, are the same astute subtleties needed by the connoisseur of fine classrooms. He advocates qualitative studies in educational research and the use of rich metaphors to describe all the intricacies in the labyrinth called a classroom. In his opinion, it is through these fertile metaphors that the real classroom comes alive.

Metaphors are like lenses.

Metaphors are comparisons that serve to illuminate the abstract and make it more concrete. Metaphors enhance understanding by giving the learner an example that is more familiar. Metaphors are like lenses: they bring the obscure into focus.

Here is one example: "He is a pillar of the community." Students know what a pillar is because they can see and touch it. Using what they know about a pillar as a comparison, they infer more about the character described as a pillar of the community—that is, someone strong, standing tall, supporting, and solid.

Why Bother?

There is no limit to the creativity of metaphorical thinking. The art and science of using metaphors is in making the abstract more concrete and making something you can't see, hear, smell, touch, or taste into something similar and familiar that you can sense in a real way.

Metaphorical thinking is a life skill.

Metaphorical thinking is a life skill that illuminates, clarifies, and radiates with deep but subtle meanings. Its usefulness and its relevance in the classroom cannot be understated.

■ □ ■ □ ■

A Tiny Transfer to Try

Birds of Transfer

Figure 1.2 introduces six birds of transfer. This exercise uses these metaphorical birds to illustrate the value of metaphors and, not just coincidentally, present different levels of transfer of learning.

TEACHER (TRAINING) TRANSFER	TRANSFER DISPOSITION	STUDENT (CLASSROOM) TRANSFER
Innovates; flies with an idea; takes ideas into action beyond the initial conception; creates; enhances; invents; risks. "You have changed my teaching forever. I can never go back to what I used to do. I know too much. I'm too excited." (Diverges)	Samantha The Soaring Eagle INNOVATES	Innovates; takes ideas beyond the initial conception; risks; diverges. *"After studying flow charts for computer class, a student constructs a Rube Goldberg type of invention."* (Innovates; invents; diverges; goes beyond and creates; has novel ideas.)
Consciously transfers ideas to various situations, contents; carries strategy as part of available repertoire; strategizes and maps. *"I use the webbing strategy in everything."* (Associates)	Cathy the Carrier Pigeon STRATEGIZES	Consciously, carries strategy to other content and situations, associates and maps. Parent-related story — *"Tina suggested we brainstorm our vacation ideas and rank them to help us decide."* (Carries new skills in life situations.)

TEACHER (TRAINING) TRANSFER	TRANSFER DISPOSITION	STUDENT (CLASSROOM) TRANSFER
Has raised consciousness, acute awareness, deliberate refinement; integrates subtly with existing repertoire. *"I haven't used any of your ideas, but I'm wording my questions carefully. I've always done this, but I'm doing more of it."* (Combines) (Persists)	Jonathan Livingston Seagull INTEGRATES	Has awareness; integrates, subtly; combines with other ideas and situations. *"I always try to guess (predict) what's gonna happen next on TV shows."* (Connects prior knowledge and experiences.)
Tailors to kids and content, but applies in similar way; all look alike; does not transfer into different situations; replicates. *"I use the web to do character analyses."* (Differentiates)	Laura The Look-alike Penguin REPLICATES	Tailors, but applies in similar situation; all look alike; replicates; meets specific needs, but goes no further. *"Paragraphing means I must have three 'indents' per page."* (Tailors with own story or essay at superficial level.)

TEACHER (TRAINING) TRANSFER	TRANSFER DISPOSITION	STUDENT (CLASSROOM) TRANSFER
Drills and practices exactly as presented; drill! drill! then stops; uses as an activity rather than as a strategy; duplicates. *"Could I have a copy of that transparency?"* (Observes)	Dan The Drilling Woodpecker DUPLICATES	Performs the drill exactly as practiced; duplicates. *"Mine is not to question why — just invert and multiply."* (No understanding of what she/he is doing)
Does nothing; unaware of relevance and misses appropriate applications; overlooks intentionally or unintentionally. *"Great session, but this won't work with my kids or content,"* or *"I chose not to use… because…"* (Persists)	Ollie The Head-in-the-Sand Ostrich OVERLOOKS	Misses appropriate opportunity; overlooks; does the same way as always. *"I get it right on the dittos, but I forget to use punctuation when I write an essay."* (Not connecting appropriateness, no application.)

Figure 1.2 Birds of transfer.

Each bird represents a kind of application done by learners as they try to use what they are learning. A learner fits a level depending on circumstances or *situational* dispositions that depend on background experiences, prior knowledge, levels of expertise, and awareness of and comfort levels with application ideas.

Set up groups of 6. Use a cooperative jigsaw to assign each member a bird from Figure 1.2 to investigate and share with the group. Emphasize the need for each investigator to decide two critical matters. First, *what* will they share about the level of transfer? What is important? What is the essence of the bird metaphor? The second critical matter is *how* will they share the information? How will they use at least three multiple intelligences to illustrate their information? Use 10 to 12 minutes to prepare and then signal groups to begin teaching each other, starting with "Ollie" and moving toward "Samantha." Discuss the relevance of knowing about transfer and why it is important to be aware of one's own transfer level in learning situations.

Analogies

A Story to Tell

A recovering alcoholic compared the recovery processes of addicts to the recovery process of a surgery patient in this way: Recovery from an addiction is to cycling in a head wind as recovery from surgery is to cycling an uphill climb. With the head wind, it goes on all day, and there seems to be no end in sight. With the uphill climb, you know there is an end point to the challenge. After you reach the top of the hill, there is relief and things get easier.

Synonyms–Analogies
related ideas
connected
direct comparisons
balance between two things
parallel ideas
pairs that match in a particular way

Things You Need to Know

What's It All About?

Analogies are comparisons based on partial similarities between like features of two things. They state a relationship and map similarities to converge on an enlightening fit. Analogies state relationships: (a) parallel part to whole (finger to hand, spoke to wheel), (b) opposites (salt to pepper, round to square), (c) object to function (gun to shoot, racket to swing), or (d) cause to effect (prosperity to happiness, success to joy).

Analogies illuminate abstract ideas by making them more concrete. Generating the inferences necessary to create and decipher analogies correctly is a highly sophisticated form of finding similarities and differences. But, remember that analogies differ from metaphors. An analogy says something is like something else, whereas a metaphor says something is something else. An analogy states a parallel; a metaphor transfers a sense of one word to another.

Analogies are like downhill skis: both work in tandem, both define and clarify a path, and both are used skillfully by experts. Figure 1.3 shows 12 templates that illustrate the relationships customarily found in analogies given in typical aptitude tests.

Analogies are like downhill skis.

CAUSE is to its EFFECT.
Example: PROSPERITY : HAPPINESS : : success : joy

ONE IMPORTANT PART is to its WHOLE.
Example: BLADE (cutting part) : KNIFE : : prong : fork

The EXTREME of one thing is to the EXTREME of another.
Example: ELATION : DEPRESSON : : acuteness : dullness

An OBJECT is to its PRIMARY FUNCTION.
Example: STOKE : HEAT : : lamp : light

A SPECIFIC ITEM is to its GENERAL CLASS.
Example: CRAB : CRUSTACEAN : : man : mammal

An OBJECT is to its CHARACTERISTIC.
Example: IRON : RIGID : : rubber : flexible

The WORD is to its SYNONYM.
Example: LUGUBRIOUS : SAD : : doleful : mournful

This WORD is to its ANTONYM.
Example: DESTITUTE : WEALTHY : : deplete : fill

This OBJECT HINDERS this ACTION.
Example: FETTER : MOVEMENT : : stutter : speech

This OBJECT ASSISTS this ACTION.
Example: VASELINE : BURN : : consolation : grief

This OBJECT is COMPOSED of this MATERIAL
Example: SHOE : LEATHER : : coat : cloth

An OBJECT is to its DEFINITION.
Example: DOGMATIC : POSITIVE : : provincial : narrow-minded

Figure 1.3 Analogy relationship templates.

Sometimes analogies fit a convergent mold as in the analogies-to-skis example. Other times, analogies imply a looser fitting comparison that lends itself to literary descriptions: "His jaw was like a steel trap"; "The moon was like a perfect croissant."

Why Bother?

The implications of this skill in the classroom reach in several directions. One direction involves students solving analogies on the multitude of tests that require analogy expertise. This may seem somewhat trite, narrow, and not very noble, but it is reality in schools today. Because testing situations occur throughout school years and well into the career years, educators would be remiss not to teach their students this skill.

Another direction is related to course content. In every subject area or discipline, analogies help to describe, clarify, and define difficult concepts. Although some people love analogy puzzles, others dread them. In either case, becoming skillful with the use of analogies will shift thinking into high gear.

Becoming skillful with the use of analogies will shift thinking into high gear.

A Tiny Transfer to Try

The Four-Fold Activity

Using cooperative groups of 3 to 5 participants, assign the usual roles: Materials Manager, Recorder, Reporter, Encourager, and Traveler. Deliver poster paper to each table and have the recorder fold it into four sections, as shown in Figure 1.4. Begin with the upper left quarter,

LIST, and continue around the other three: RANK, COMPARE, and ILLUSTRATE.

LIST	RANK
(Brainstorm 20-30 synonyms)	(Prioritize the top 3)
COMPARE (___is to ____as ___is to____, because both 1___, 2___, 3___) (Analogy)	ILLUSTRATE (Create a poster or visual metaphor of your analogy comparison)

Figure 1.4 Four-fold activity.

Discuss specific applications for teachers to use with this four-fold activity.

Family of Strategies: Summarizing and Note-taking (2SN)

Strategies

Summarizing

Note-taking

 **Summarizing**

A Story to Tell

A coed remembers the time when she borrowed a text from a college classmate, when they were both doctoral students at Loyola University in Chicago. She had missed some classes and was hoping that her friend had highlighted the important parts in the chapters, with a florescent marker, thus summarizing succinctly the key ideas. However, the coed noticed that those highlighted parts highlighted everything. There were page after page of brightly colored patterns with entire paragraphs glowing.

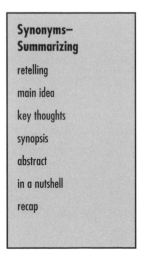

Synonyms— Summarizing
retelling
main idea
key thoughts
synopsis
abstract
in a nutshell
recap

When she returned the book, she kidded her colleague about the abundance of highlights, to which her friend replied, "It all seems important, so I just keep highlighting."

Things You Need to Know

What's It All About?

Summarizing is putting ideas in your own words after reading something or listening to someone. Summarizing, which is not the same as plagiarizing, is using your own words to crystallize the essence of an idea presented. Good summarizing does not copy exactly the words or phrases from the printed page or the spoken word. It is "a taste" of a hearty and robust idea—sampling but not consuming the entire meal. Or, in another comparison, summarizing is like a haiku—both take a long, winding thought and distill the essence through a few well-chosen words.

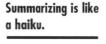

Summarizing is like a haiku.

Summarizing skill requires tacit understanding and skillful compacting of the idea to be condensed in order to present a succinct synopsis that captures the essence of the whole. For example, students might be asked to summarize a news event into a few sentences, or a "sound bite" in contemporary terms. Although summaries are simple recollections of a larger piece, they do call for skilled inclusion and exclusion of facts.

The skill of summarizing is a life skill that helps people avoid using the "short version" of the bed-to-bed stories that permeate many conversations. In a typical bed-to-bed narrative, the speaker says, "I got up. I ate breakfast.

Next, I had lunch. Then, I had dinner and finally, I went to bed." Or, they say, "He was born. He lived here in his youth. He moved there. Then, he moved again. He worked. He married. He had three children. He retired and bought a hobby farm. And then he died."

These are not very helpful summaries. Rather than selecting the high points of interest, the speaker or writer tells and retells at length and in detail the sequence of every event that happened.

Why Bother?

The skill of summarizing—being able to come away from a learning experience and identify the gist of it—is vital to effective learning. It is what good readers do to make meaning of a text, whether they are long and windy nonfiction pieces or flowing literary language in works of fiction. It is what good students do, too.

> **Summarizing is what good readers do to make meaning of a text.**

A Tiny Transfer to Try

2-4-8 Focus Interview

Introduce the following problem as a focus for the exercise with participants.

> What is the day after the day after tomorrow, if the day before the day before yesterday was Monday?

Have participants work individually to solve the problem, and, after they have an answer, ask them to begin the 2-4-8 Focus Interview process by finding a partner and discussing their solution and strategies. Then, go through the steps in order—2-4-8.

Two

In pairs, Partners A and B share their solution and strategies with an artifact (a piece of paper or problem) in hand. They listen intently, ask questions of each other, try to understand exactly what the greatest challenges were, and look at what worked and what didn't. After both have shared, they find another pair ready to talk.

Four

Now, in the foursome, each person tells the partner's story about the problem-solving. It's time to see how well each listened and how well they can summarize the essence of the partner interaction. When all four have had a turn, the foursome looks for another foursome to join to make eight.

Eight

Again, in this interaction, the members of the groups tell a different story by summarizing a third story. The focus is on the strategies used. This encourages summarizing at its core. When finished, ask students about their thoughts on the process of the 2-4-8 Focus Interview—what did they like and what did they think was hard.

Note-taking

A Story to Tell

In a similar experience to the borrowed college text, the same coed asked to use her friend's set of class notes from the previous night's session. Her reactions to the borrowed notes fit into the range of personal reactions others have had in similar situations. She was amazed at how complete the notes were and how every detail seemed to be there.

As she looked at the sprawling writing style, she kept thinking about her own notes, which usually looked more like a neat and tidy outline, sprinkled with bulleted points. Her notes often had doodles connecting and framing key words and phrases. As she started to copy the borrowed set of notes, she couldn't help thinking about how highly personal note-taking is, tailored by and to the note-taker.

Synonyms—Note-taking
notation
memos
shorthand
outline
lists
bullet points
summaries
personal interpretations
outlining
key phrases
jottings
personal notations
key words
reminders

Things You Need to Know

What's It All About?

Note-taking is the act of selecting ideas from a text or presentation to record in brief form. Its purpose is to hone the essence of an idea into a few chosen words to spark remembrance and understanding of the bigger idea it represents. Note-taking is a skill that summarizes or captures the main ideas about a topic. Note-taking is like fingerprinting: both the notes and the fingerprints are unique to the person, represent a part of the person, and are lasting impressions that others might share.

Note-taking is like fingerprinting.

Note-taking is used during oral presentations and during reading. As suggested in the story, the notes might be written narratives, brief outlines, random phrases, sketches, or diagrams. In addition, graphic organizers, such as mind maps and fishbone diagrams, are helpful tools for note-taking.

Notes from a lecture on photosynthesis could be taken in a number of styles and might look like the examples in Figures 2.1, 2.2 and 2.3.

Photosynthesis CO_2 (Carbon dioxide) H_2O (water)

Plants **take in** nutrients: water, sunlight, and CO_2

Plants **put out** oxygen.

Photosynthesis is part of the life cycle.

Figure 2.1 Note-taking style: outline of key phrases.

Plants manufacture carbohydrates, and oxygen as a by-product, which is given off from the plant into the atmosphere. To make oxygen and carbohydrates, plants need nutrients: water (H_2O), carbon dioxide (CO_2), and sunlight. The sunlight provides the energy needed for this process. This cycle of plants taking in sunlight, minerals, carbon dioxide, and water to manufacture carbohydrates and release oxygen gas is part of the life cycle in the food chain.

Figure 2.2 Note-taking style: narrative.

An example of this theory at work is mediated journals (Feuerstein, 1980), which label pages prior to the learning as a signal to the note-taker of what is important. For example, the note-taker uses one piece of paper folded in half to make a four-page Journal, labelled as shown:

Title		H_2O	CO_2		Photosyn-thesis
1		2	3		4

Figure 2.3 Note-taking style: graphic organizer.

Why Bother?

It is hard to understate the implications of note-taking as a tool for learning. Just in the act of writing, even if the notes are never read or looked at again, muscle memory is at work. This powerful memory technique, located in the cerebellum, is one of the most striking parts of the memory system. Muscle memory works to groove the motions in a golf swing or a tennis serve, and it works to imprint on the mind the word and images recorded by large and small muscle groups.

> **Just in the act of writing, even if the notes are never read or looked at again, muscle memory is at work.**

A Tiny Transfer to Try

Mediated Journal

Develop the idea of a "mediated journal" to scaffold the skill of note-taking. Set up a journal with headings prior to the start of the unit. Decide on how many pages are needed and on how to organize the page headings to signal what is important for students to capture. Work in A-B pairs.

Here is an example of labels used for a sixth-grade science unit on the human body. Each group of students has a vital organ of the body to study and to defend in a simulation with the "Human Body Corporation" that is threatening to fire parts of the body in a cost-cutting strategy. Figure 2.4 shows some of the headings chosen for the student journals.

Cover	Labeled Diagram of the organ (two page spread)
Definition	
Terminology	Persuasive letter to the corporate leadership, defending the organ
Problem Statement (for Problem Based Learning)	Resources
KND Chart (two page spread Know, Need to Know, Need to Do for investigation)	

Figure 2.4 Example journal headings.

Notice how a heading serves as advance organizer or anticipatory guide, giving students a preview of what is coming in the unit. This strategy is discussed more fully in chapter 9 on Questions and Cues and Advanced Organizers.

Family of Strategies: Reinforcing Effort and Providing Recognition (3RR)

Strategies

Reinforcing Effort

Providing Recognition

 **Reinforcing Effort**

A Story to Tell

"Where were you stuck and how did you get unstuck?" These were the words of one committee member during a doctoral dissertation oral defense. The doctoral candidate was stunned by the fact that the professor somehow knew she had been stuck. It was not something she had expected to happen at that point in her journey toward a Ph.D.

She wondered aloud how she knew she had been stuck and he laughed and said, "Everyone gets stuck! It's part of the process." Of course,

Synonyms—Reinforcing Effort
encouraging
supporting
defining
recognizing
acknowledging
noticing
pointing out
emphasizing

she had no previous understanding of that and had been careful not to let her committee know how stuck she was. She was afraid they might make her start over or do more or go in another direction. Yet, when she thinks about the "lessons learned" during her doctoral studies, she often thinks of this incident and what she learned about her own problem-solving methods.

Things You Need to Know

What's It All About?

Reinforcing effort is acknowledging student work, whether it is successful or not so successful attempts. The point is to notice the effort that the student has exerted and to motivate that student to progress further. Reinforcing effort is not to be confused with continuous and unending praise that is simply part and parcel of some classroom rhetoric, but rather is genuine reinforcement of efforts exhibited. Reinforcing effort is like vigorously and regularly polishing a car with a fine wax coating. Both the reinforcing behaviors and the wax coating strengthen existing elements; the regular and consistent exercise itself demonstrates the value placed on on-going durable effort, and a resulting glow is observable with both.

Reinforcing effort is like vigorously and regularly polishing a car with a fine wax coating.

In the early grades, if teachers choose to demonstrate reinforcement by awarding stickers, stars, and smiley faces, reinforcement is most effective if they reinforce the actual effort evidenced in the process as well as rewarding the final product or good work that resulted. It is in reinforcing effort that students learn the lessons of precision, persistence, and pride.

■ □ ■ □ ■

It is important to note that the research suggests that symbolic recognition works better than tangible rewards. On the basketball court, the encouraging pat on the back from the coach as the player returns to the bench shows appreciation for the effort. The quiet efforts of a well-executed chemistry lab experiment may be applauded with a private comment from the science teacher. "You did a great job today with the acids and bases experiments. I really appreciate the care you showed in your laboratory technique for preventing contamination." These two examples impy that the use of reinforcing behavior impacts positively on the learners and that it encourages continuing, consistent, and conscious efforts.

Why Bother?

Students seem most responsive when positive reinforcement is married to predictable consequences in classroom management. In terms of academic work, the positive reinforcement that is most empowering is feedback that is specific, immediate, and genuine.

In terms of academic work, the positive reinforcement that is most empowering is feedback that is specific, immediate, and genuine.

Although it is important to distinguish the difference between intrinsic and extrinsic motivation, this best practice focuses on explicit attention to teaching about motivation. It is imperative in lifelong learning that students become self-initiating and self-motivated learners. The more they learn about themselves and their strengths and weaknesses, the more they will manage ably this aspect of learning.

The overriding implication of reinforcing effort in schooling is in the value placed on the process by paying explicit attention to it. It is by teaching students about the process that they learn how to preserve and complete projects. The real power in reinforcing effort is talking to students about the processes of working through a problem or project, being challenged, becoming frustrated, struggling with a particularly troubling aspect, and feeling that sense of accomplishment when success is at hand. The implication is for teachers to use reinforcement strategies skillfully and with real purpose to foster lifelong habits of mind.

A Tiny Transfer to Try

Mrs. Poindexter's Prompts

Use A-B pairs. Ask the following questions, which are Mrs. Poindexter's prompts: "When did you get stuck? How did you get unstuck?" Members are to tell personal stories of a time when they were stuck—really stuck—on a problem and how they got unstuck. Discuss the power of knowing that "getting stuck" is part of the process in challenging tasks and how teachers and students might reinforce effort by acknowledging that phenomenon more frequently.

Discuss how you might introduce Mrs. Poindexter's prompts to your students and how you might incorporate them into class or cooperative learning reflections.

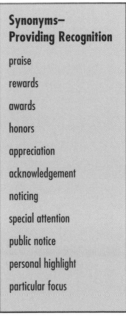 Providing Recognition

A Story to Tell

As the first grade students shared their portfolios with their parents, one little guy showed a photo of himself from a field trip. His reflection was, "I was the muddiest!"

His Mom stopped him and said, "What did you say?"

He repeated proudly, "I was the muddiest! The teacher said that I was the muddiest of anyone she had ever seen."

Although this may not be the kind of academic recognition parents usually want, this anecdote does illustrate the power of a teacher's words on students.

**Synonyms—
Providing Recognition**

praise

rewards

awards

honors

appreciation

acknowledgement

noticing

special attention

public notice

personal highlight

particular focus

Things You Need to Know

What's It All About?

In the context of this work, the authors define the concept of recognition as praise, rewards, awards, or teacher acknowledgment to students for some accomplishment. Recognition may be informal or formal, and it may involve tangibles or intangibles. Contrasting the ideas of recognition and reinforcement, these synonyms for recognition come to mind: acknowledge, appreciate, note, or value.

Recognition is like a chair: both provide observable structure to the learner, both add support as the learner tires, and both become more comfortable and reliable over time. Chairs are as integral to the suite of office furniture as recognition is integral to the suite of teaching behaviors.

Recognition is like a chair.

Recognition is the teacher's acknowledgment of student effort, such as a well-stated opinion, a completed academic task, a submitted project, a drafted proposal, or a final comprehensive product. It may take the form of informal verbal comments, such as "Nice job on your outline" or "I like the way you stated your opinion so succinctly," to more formal forms of recognition, such as a certificate of achievement or a published list of names honoring some effort. Recognition is epitomized on the football field by the cheers of the crowd when a great play is completed and also by the generous applause of the crowd when an injured player is taken off the field.

According to Marzano, Pickering, and Pollock (2001), research in recognition suggests that students' attitudes and beliefs impact their achievement. When teachers help students see the connection between effort and achievement, students better understand the relationship between the two and develop more positive attitudes. They see that putting in the effort reaps positive results: good grades, higher achievement, peer recognition, and more formal teacher recognition. This discussion and the activities included here follow that vein of thought.

However, please note that there are two sides to this issue, and a number of notable voices question the effects of praise, rewards, and recognition. Among the early writers in this area is Mary Budd Rowe (1974), a science educator who contends that when teachers constantly praise students and indiscriminately offer rewards, student thinking is compromised and student responses remain at lower levels of critical analysis and creative ideation.

> **there are two sides to [the recognition]... issue.**

Another dissenting voice in the field is Alfie Kohn, educator, debater, and author of *Punished by Rewards* (1993), who believes that when praising one student, other students are emotionally impacted.

In addition, Jensen (1996) distinguishes the idea of rewards and recognition as they relate to intrinsic and extrinsic motivation. Jensen explains that it is best to eliminate rewards for good behavior, attendance, and completed homework because the extrinsic reward system causes anxiety and uncertainty in the brain. In research studies in the laboratory on brain functions, more often than not the rewarded behavior stops as soon as the reward stops. Instead, Jensen suggests that teachers use alternatives: acknowledgement, celebrations, and increased variety and quantity of feedback.

Why Bother?

The implications of this strategy impact directly on the learning environment. Recognition is another key to "classroom instruction that works," according to the authors of the book by that same name. Recognition, as distinguished from reinforcement, means being

---
**Recognition...
means being
acknowledged.**

---

acknowledged through praise, rewards, and awards for something. Implied in that acknowledgment is an appreciation of student thinking.

A Tiny Transfer to Try

The Human Graph

Everyone's idea counts! One way to recognize or acknowledge students is through the use of the human graph (see Figure 3.1) in which each student becomes part of a class graph. By choosing to take a "public stand"—stating an opinion and supporting the opinion with a justifying statement—each student is recognized as having an important idea to share. Use a whole group interaction for this activity.

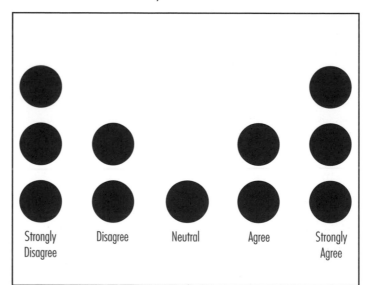

Figure 3.1 Human graph.

Step 1: Take a Stand!

Ask participants to line up on the imaginary line in response to one of the following cueing statements:

> 1. Teacher evaluation is linked to student achievement.
>
> 2. About the human brain, I know... (A lot, A little, Don't know, Not Much, Next to Nothing)
>
> 3. Would you rather be: Fraction/Decimal; Noun/Verb; Fiction/Nonfiction; Island/Peninsula, Hard Data or Soft Data.

Step 2: Justify!

Talk about the concept of gathering, analyzing, and interpreting data and how the human graph helps that focus. Sample some statements of fact that tell what the graph represents and talk about quantitative terms, such as *some, a few, many, the majority, no one.*

Then, look at the reasons and different lines of thought that are represented. Encourage attentive listening and movement on the graph if people change their minds as they hear a differing viewpoint.

In another classroom application, make puppets to repeat the human graph on a wall graph. Each student has a self-puppet to attach on one of five strips of Velcro to match the line on the human graph. Students can put the information from the graphs into a computer graphing program and print out the class graphs on various topics.

In this way, students are immersed in the concept of graphing data from a concrete, human graph to a representational picture graph, to an abstract printed graph. With lots of applications of their process in the classroom, students become very familiar with the use of graphs and data.

Family of Strategies: Homework and Practice (4HP)

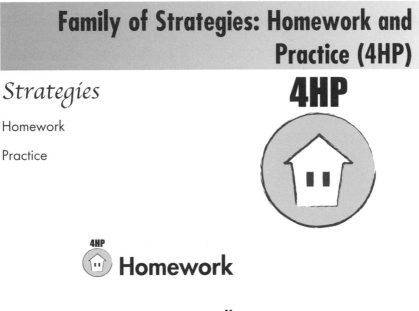

Strategies

Homework

Practice

4HP

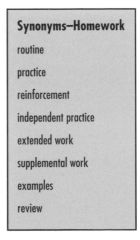

4HP
🏠 Homework

A Story to Tell

During a short flight from Singapore to Malaysia, a proud Malaysian father told the woman seated next to him the story of his son's recent graduation from high school and that his son was off to an engineering school in the United States. As the story was winding down, he ended with the statement, "He had a perfect score on our national mathematics test."

Astonished by the idea of a perfect mathematics score on a test of that sort, the woman asked him, "How does one get a perfect score on a mathematics test of that stature?"

Synonyms–Homework
routine
practice
reinforcement
independent practice
extended work
supplemental work
examples
review

His reply described a system that is typical in that part of the world. He explained, "Students study very hard in our country. They go to school all day and then, following their regular school, they work with tutors in special 'after school' schools. They spend many hours reviewing the material from the day, practicing the exercises, and repeating the program content in an effort to repeat and recite the material by rote memory and by multiple applications."

As he talked, the woman was reminded of a parallel story from a previous visit to Singapore. In this story, the hosting educator invited the woman to her home. As they walked around the beautiful split-level dwelling, she pointed to a smallish room just off the dining area. It was lined with book shelves and had a large table in the center of the space. She explained, "This is the tutor's room. We decided we needed to devote a room for the children so they could do their homework in a formal setting. The tutor works with them every day right after school. They spend several hours, at least, working on their school work and learning their mother tongue, the Manderin language."

Things You Need to Know

What's It All About?

Homework consists of schoolwork that is done at home after the regular school day or during the weekend. It may be assigned by the teacher, or it may be unfinished schoolwork the student chooses to complete at home. Traditionally, homework is either a review and practice of skills being learned or additional, independent work, such as a project, that requires more time than is available during the school day.

Homework might focus on drill and repeated or patterned exercises (multiplication tables) to learn how to do a needed skill. It might mean a robust project (science fair project) that needs extended time and materials from the home front. Homework might involve teamwork with partners (an art collage) or it might be a long-term effort that extends through the semester or term (research paper). Yet, most often, homework is a daily chore connected to the schoolwork of that day (textbook exercises or work sheets).

Homework is as old as the hills. Most parents and students are as familiar with the concept of homework as teachers are. Homework involves assignment notebooks, textbooks, papers, notes and work sheets carried back and forth perhaps in backpacks. It *always* involves time and energy. It *sometimes* involves dialogue with another for some needed help. And, it *occasionally* involves "blood, sweat, and tears" to get the homework finished. Homework is like the chore of doing the laundry. Both are daily or weekly recurring events, both require time and energy to do, both get easier the more often you do them, and both leave you with a sense of accomplishment and closure...something got done!

Walberg's (1999) metaphor of a three-legged stool comes to mind as part of the body of research that supports this best practice. In the metaphor, school is like a three-legged stool: the three legs are the student, teacher, and parent, all playing a critical role in the success of the student. Of course, students have the primary role here.

School is like a three-legged stool.

■ □ ■ □ ■

They are the ones that must carry out the tasks. Teachers must share their expectations, rules, and routines concerning homework with both students and parents. Parents, then, must support the policies and practices that the teachers outline. That does not mean doing the homework with the student. It does mean helping their children to develop homework routines that work: setting a regular time, making it a priority over other things, creating a place conducive to doing the homework, acknowledging the importance of homework, and holding students accountable for doing it with care and completion. Only when all three legs are in place will the stool stand.

Why Bother?

The more time [students]... study, the better they understand their subject matter.

The bottom line is that homework extends the school day and the amount of time students work on their studies. The more time they study, the better they understand their subject matter. The implications of homework on student achievement are captured in the story about how the Asian culture values homework. It's that simple.

A Tiny Transfer to Try

Homework Tales

Tell the following two "Homework Tales"

Tale Number 1

The story of Izzy, as told by John Barell, is about the Nobel prize-winning physicist, I. I. Rabi. When asked why he became a scientist, Dr. Rabi told the story of how his mother would always ask him the same question. He said, "She never asked me what I did that day. She never asked who I was with. She always asked the very same thing. My Mom would say, 'Izzy, did you ask a good question, today?' And, I think that is why I went into the field of science inquiry."

Tale Number 2

At a conference on early literacy, one panel member advised parents that the most beneficial thing they could do to foster reading in their youngsters was to read to them every day. She emphasized the *every day* part.

Following the panel presentations, parents were encouraged to ask questions and to dialogue with the panel members. A concerned parent stood up and asked, "Do we have to read to our kids *every day* (also emphasizing the *every day* part)?"

The distinguished speaker replied, "Oh, no, of course not. You don't have to read to your child every day...only on the days that you eat!"

After sharing these two tales, work in small teams to complete the t-chart in Figure 4.1 for parents. Include specific ways parents can facilitate the completion of routine, skill-and-drill homework as well as homework that involves the creation of a quality project.

To Do	Not To Do

Figure 4.1 Homework: to do or not to do.

 Practice

A Story to Tell

There is a story about how Tiger Woods became the youngest and greatest golfer in the world. It's about the practice routine his dad set up for him, beginning at the age of three. Tiger learned the game of golf from " the hole out." That is, he practiced starting at the hole and moving toward the tee, rather than the traditional way of starting at the tee and working out to the hole on the putting green. He learned to putt toward the goal (in golf, a small hole in the ground) from a foot away, then from two feet away, and continued moving away from the hole in

Synonyms—Practices
rehearsal
repetition
skill-and-drill repetition
repeated use
tries
trials
patterned exercises
extended school work

■□■□■

small increments until he was skilled and confident in making long putts on the green.

Then, he began chipping from a few feet off the green, which gave him practice in using his short irons, considered the easier of the golfing tools. Gradually, his dad increased the distance so the chips became pitches using the longer irons. Eventually, Tiger learned to use his fairway woods (another set of tools), and finally, he had worked his way all the way back to the tee, where he would practice with the longest hitting club, the driver. With continual, consistent, and coached practice, rehearsal, and repetition, Tiger became a skilled and winning junior golfer and, as the saga continues, is setting major records in his first years of joining the professional golf tour.

Things You Need You to Know

What's It All About?

Guided practice and independent practice are both part of this picture. Guided practice is mediated by the teacher, whereas independent practice is "on your own," and often is manifested in homework assignments. Practice entails focus and concentration on a skill, problem, or project that occurs beyond the formal classroom input mode. Practice is the exercise that is done to repeat what is being studied in a way that fosters either rote memory or deep understanding.

Rote learning is practicing the times tables, over and over and over again, until they are automatic, while deep understanding is achieved through the repeated practice of writing adverbial phrases in a creative writing assignment. Practice is serving the tennis ball 10, 15, or 25 times until the serve is "grooved." It is working on the piano scales every day after school, until the fingering is so automatic the fingers fly across the keys. Practice is doing something so many times that it becomes part of an automatic repertoire that is done with skill and grace.

These practices, whether guided or independent, provide the kind of extended learning needed for students to know, understand, retain, and recall key information and life skills. Coached practices and self-initiated independent exercises are needed to perform dance routines, football plays, or academic presentations at competent and proficient levels. Practice is like a journey: both have a beginning and end, both take unexpected turns, and both are memorable over time. Practice can be a trip over a routine, well-worn path, or it can be a run into new territory, taking a different or unknown path.

Practice is like a journey.

It is a well-known fact that talent does not always lead to the winning edge. The difference between proficient and expert performances often depends on the amount and quality of practice. Some say, "Practice makes perfect," whereas others correct that comment and say, "Practice makes permanent." Still others prefer to say, "Perfect practice makes perfect."

Why Bother?

Much of school learning comprises rote memory, automated skills, and explicitly learned facts and data. To retain these kinds of information requires practice, rehearsal, and repetition. Practice provides the polish to write with clarity and elegance, to read with fluency and ease, and to speak with wisdom and grace. Practice moves the learner from novice to advanced beginner to competent user to proficient user, and, finally, to expert.

Thus, the implication is that effective teachers include purposeful practice in their instructional design. They know how, when, and how much practice is appropriate and build practice into every lesson of substance. Effective teachers understand that students need extended time to work with many of the skills and ideas introduced in a crowded curriculum and they take advantage of the power of practice.

> **Effective teachers include purposeful practice in their instructional design.**

A Tiny Transfer to Try

Practice Routines and Personal Regimens

In A-B pairs, review the list of categories and the sample types of repeated practices that are typical within each category shown in Figure 4.2. Then, name a skill from one of the listed categories or from your own life experiences. Describe your practice regimen by drawing a sequence chart or flow chart (see Figure 4.3) of the various steps or phases in the routine. Tell what helps motivate you to practice often and with focused attention to what you are doing.

Using the scenario shared with your partner, describe a *mental rehearsal exercise* that you can include as part of the practice and rate the effect it could have on your overall skill development.

Sport drills: tennis serve, basketball free throw, golf swing, lifting weights, aerobic workout

Course work exercises: keyboarding, drafting, Palm Pilot draw feature

Practical skills: Driving a car, chopping vegetables, knitting, crocheting, gardening, painting

Fine Arts: Piano, oil painting, acting, singing, sculpting, pottery making

Figure 4.2 Practice categories.

Figure 4.3 Flow chart.

Family of Strategies: Nonlinguistic Representations (5NR)

Strategies

5NR

Multiple Intelligences

Drawings

Graphic Organizers

Physical/Mental Models

 **Multiple Intelligences**

A Story to Tell

At a summer workshop for teachers on principles and practices that work for the K-12 classroom, the instructor took an informal survey of the years of experience represented by the teachers in the room. People raised their hands for 1 year, 5 years, 10 years, 20 years, and so on until the number hit 35 years. Then, someone yelled out 43 years! Wow! Naturally, everyone applauded, and the woman stood up and took a bow. She said, "I've been at this a long time. I'm an old English teacher. How many of you remember diagramming sentences?"

**Synonyms—
Multiple Intelligences**

talents

abilities

capabilities

potentialities

expertise

skillfulness

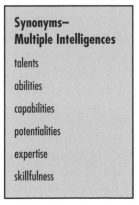

Lots of teachers responded to that question with hands waving high. Then the veteran teacher asked, "How many of you like diagramming sentences?"

To the surprise of many, over two-thirds of the hands remained high in the air. People started commenting on the how much they "loved" doing the diagrams and how they had learned about the parts of speech and sentence structure and punctuation in ways that they have never forgotten. They raved about how visual the exercise of diagramming was and how it helped the learner see sentences more clearly.

Finally, the seasoned English teacher asked, "How many of you have your students diagram sentences, today? When not a single hand went up, she said, "Sometimes we forget the power of simple visual tools."

Things You Need You to Know

What's It All About?

The theory of multiple intelligences is formally defined as the suite of differing and skillful ways to solve problems and create products that are valued by a culture. In a less formal definition, multiple intelligences comprise the talents and abilities of human beings that reflect a different profile of strengths in each person.

The ultimate framework that provides opportunity for nonlinguistic representations of ideas is embodied in Howard Gardner's theory of multiple intelligences. Gardner (1983, 1991) first presented his theory of multiple intelligences in 1983 and modified it in 1991.

Now, the theory posits eight ways of knowing: visual, verbal, interpersonal, intrapersonal, mathematical, musical, naturalist, and bodily (V-V-I-I-M-M-N-B). Using multiple intelligences theory, teachers have a framework to think about multiple ways to *present* information and to consider multiple ways for students to *express* what they know. For example, allowing students to create a model of the life cycle illustrates in nonlinguistic terms the same information that might be written in an expository essay. Encouraging students to represent their understanding of democracy through a visual metaphor or political cartoon or through a written expose, are examples of how multiple intelligences plays out in the classroom.

Multiple intelligences are like novels: both come in a variety of flavors, a spectrum of sizes, a variety of settings and themes and both create a profile for the individual. Multiple intelligences theory is, metaphorically, a library of novels from the mundane to the magnificent. Each volume presents a particular view of the world.

> **Multiple intelligences are like novels.**

Why Bother?

The implications of multiple intelligences theory are central to both the teaching and learning processes. Gardner's framework provides the perfect tool for the diverse and multicultural classrooms of today's schools. Using the eight multiple intelligences means creating lessons using at least three intelligences that are differentiated for the various learners and the various learning styles in the classroom. Differentiation means to teach or re-teach in a new and

> **Gardner's framework provides the perfect tool for the diverse and multicultural classrooms of today's schools.**

different way—try a visual, use a physical model, have students role play, or use music as the channel of choice.

A Tiny Transfer to Try

Gallery Smarts

This exercise surveys the community resources that support the development of the multiple intelligences. Before the lesson, post eight large sheets of paper on the walls around the room. Organize in small groups by having the participants line up and count off by eight. Ask each group to find the poster paper with their number on it. Explain that the task is to create a list of multiple intelligences activities and experiences that fit with the target intelligence and are available in the community, nearby cities, or region. Explain that these lists are to be used to create a community brochure for parents to use during vacations and holidays as a resource guide of things to do in the area. Have each team list two items on the poster.

Then, in a gallery walk or carousel, have the teams move to the next poster (move counter-clockwise about the room). Discuss the highlights when all teams have completed the entire eight posters in the carousel. Talk about how this step builds to a completed brochure project, using graphic arts, computers, and copiers in the world of electronic technology.

Drawings

A Story to Tell

There are students who prefer to draw or sketch their ideas, rather than write them. They have a more visual interpretation of the world around them. One vivid example of this phenomenon is epitomized in a sixth-grade boy who was able to represent a deep understanding of the human skeletal system through his drawing. He was the appointed recorder in his cooperative group. As he prepared to start recording the information on the large poster paper, the girl next to him grabbed the marker and said, "I'll be the recorder. You can't write and you can't spell." The savvy teacher happened by just at that moment. As she took the marker from the girl and handed it to the boy, she said, "He's the recorder."

The newly affirmed recorder created an absolutely exquisite drawing of the human skeleton, complete with ball and sockets, a rib cage, and jointed appendages on both hands and both feet. The image was rich in detail, perfectly proportioned and vividly displayed. As the girl added the labels to the diagram, this wise teacher allowed the collaboration. Needless to say, it was one of the most accurate and definitely the most dramatic student presentation of deep understanding.

Synonyms–Drawings

pictures

sketches

doodles

images

visual

representations

Things You Need You to Know

What's It All About?

Drawings are sketches that represent ideas in non-linguistic ways. A picture is worth a thousand words, wisdom says. One drawing can efficiently and effectively deliver much information without words. Graphically represented ideas become concrete images that show rather than tell. Drawings are preferred by some visually oriented students, and they are the modus operandi for some teachers. Drawings, sketches, and cartoons all enhance understanding through images and pictures of ideas that clarify and define.

Drawings are like flowers.

Drawings are like flowers: both have simple beginnings, both blossom into complex designs, and both are appreciated by others. Try explaining one of the following figures and then notice how succinctly the picture relays the message (see Figures 5.1 and 5.2).

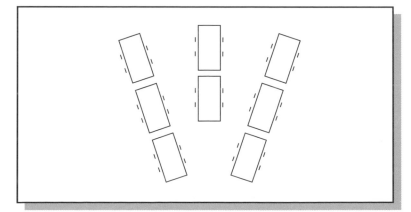

Figure 5.1 Tables arranged in "v" to the front.

Figure 5.2 Tip of the iceberg metaphor.

Why Bother?

The implication here is simple and well-known to teachers. Students need ample opportunities to use pictures, drawings, and sketches as ways to depict their thinking. They need ample materials to foster the creative, elaborate, and detailed drawings to represent in-depth thinking about the idea. Cartoons, comics, illustrations, labeled diagrams, and scale drawings all fall into this category of visual intelligence.

> **Students need ample opportunities to use pictures, drawings, and sketches as ways to depict their thinking.**

A Tiny Transfer to Try

Art Journals

This exercise uses drawings to depict information. Work in partners to create a four-page art journal of the workshop. Use drawings, symbols, and sketches to tell the story of the day. Share with a partner pair, and then discuss an appropriate opportunity to use an art journal assignment in the classroom.

5NR Graphic Organizers

A Story to Tell

A professor asked his graduate student to depict several boxes of data on a single sheet of paper. The student laughed at the thought of trying to reduce all of her notes for her dissertation to a graphic of one page, but as she tackled what seemed like a daunting task, she started to understand the power of graphic displays.

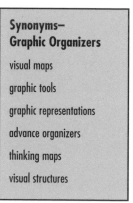

**Synonyms—
Graphic Organizers**

visual maps

graphic tools

graphic representations

advance organizers

thinking maps

visual structures

To her genuine surprise, a coherent graphic emerged from her struggles, yet another testimony to the concept of nonlinguistic representation.

Things You Need to Know

What's It All About?

Graphic organizers are visual tools that are used to represent different kinds of information. They sort and order ideas in the same way as outlining. The widespread use of graphic organizers, such as mind *maps*, *flow charts*, and *attribute webs*, provides visual tools or, as Hyerle (1996) calls them, thinking maps, for students to "see" their thinking. These visuals aid in the analysis and synthesis of *new* information and the clarification and focus of more *familiar* information.

Miles and Huberman (1984) discuss the concept of nonlinguistic representations of qualitative research data and refer to them as visual displays. Lyman and McTighe (1988) discuss the idea of theory-embedded tools such as graphic organizers. Hyerle (1996) designates specific kinds of thinking for particular kinds of maps.

Graphic organizers can be used to gather information— from a text, a video presentation, a lecture, or an Internet search—or to represent a personal interpretation of an idea, with connections specific to the person's viewpoint. Individual students can employ the graphic tools to capture the essence of an idea in notes or in a work sample. Displayed on large newsprint as part of a cooperative task, graphic tools foster lively conversation and critical analysis of work by giving the cooperative team the ability to manipulate their emerging ideas so that all can see and review them.

For example, asking students to do a concept map of their perception of a video on memory and learning provides ripe opportunities for deep understanding and reflective insights. Seeing the picture of their thinking enhances the connections they make.

To think about graphic organizers in yet another way, graphic organizers are like perennials: both begin as a simple bulb, both bloom into full and flowing flowers, and both capture the essence of the final product.

Graphic organizers are like perennials.

After students have been introduced to the "magic" three—attribute web, right angle thinking, and fishbone (discussed next)—the next step is to have students do the choosing. As they pick the graphic most appropriate for their material or their intended use of the material, they can reflect about the criteria for choosing the most useful graphic for a particular situation. The selection process causes a metacognitive leap for students because it is not only empowering but also instructive in the analyses they need to make to select the appropriate graphic.

Although there are myriad graphic organizers and visual maps available for use in the K-12 classroom, the authors have selected three simple, versatile, and frequently used graphic organizers as "the magic three" to demonstrate this best practice of non-linguistic representations: attribute web, fishbone, and flow chart. However, be aware that in addition to these three and other published graphic organizers, learners may also create their own graphic to display their information.

Attribute Web. The attribute web is a convergent thinking process that serves to analyze and pinpoint the various characteristic or traits of an object or idea (Figure 5.3). It calls for careful evaluation, analysis, and dissecting of ideas to find the discriminating elements that compose the whole. The center of the web contains the focus idea, and the webbed spokes spring out from the central idea, naming and labeling the different elements. The process helps illuminate the component parts of the entirety.

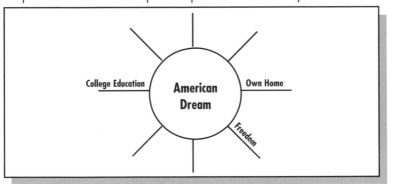

Figure 5.3 Attribute web.

Right Angle Thinking. If you are a fan of reflective thinking and metacognitive, learning-to-learn tools, this graphic organizer tops the list (Figure 5.4). It is the kind of thinking that often leads to peripheral discoveries that are not the targeted focus of the investigation while working on one idea, another idea occurs. It is how penicillin was discovered. It's about noticing something that is occurring and making note of it in a formal way, capturing the related thought for future exploration. Right angle thinking calls for two different kinds of thinking. One kind involves the skills of summarizing, finding the main idea, and writing a synopsis of the findings. The other kind calls for a reflective stance of connecting ideas, capturing related thoughts, and jotting down a stray thought that occurs.

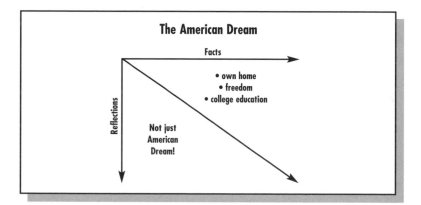

Figure 5.4 Right angle thinking.

Fishbone. Introduced through the formal brainstorming techniques of Edward Deming's Quality Management Theory (1986), the fishbone (Figure 5.5) is a perfect analysis tool that leads students toward the more formal Harvard outline. The fishbone has four parts: the head of the fish or the goal, the spine to represent an overriding theme that runs through the idea, ribs that capture the subheadings, and "riblets" for the details about the information on each rib. Sorting, categorizing, labeling the various ribs and filling in any details that come to mind involve many higher order thinking skills: analyzing, evaluating, judging, deciding, and classifying. Students can easily create a more formal outline from the fishbone analysis.

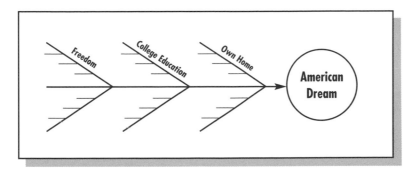

Figure 5.5 Fishbone.

Why Bother?

> **Graphic organizers tap into the visual intelligence of the learner.**

Graphic organizers tap into the visual intelligence of the learner. They also have implications for higher order thinking, and can, in fact, facilitate all kinds of critical and creative thinking just by the nature of their structures. Some organizers call for generation of ideas, whereas others call for analysis and evaluation of ideas. Thus, the skillful and frequent use of the different graphic tools encourages both the synthesis and the analysis of information.

A Tiny Transfer to Try

The Magic Three Carousel

This exercise introduces and uses three graphic tools to analyze and represent information. Work in groups of 3 to 4. Ask teams to each use a different graphic to represent the same information about types of music. The task is to unpack their graphic about types of music and prepare a presentation that includes four points: a completed example of the graphic; applications for mathematics, science, language arts, and social studies; guidelines for using the graphic effectively; and a jingle or rap that portrays the power of the graphic organizer. Discuss the pros and cons of each of the three graphics for depicting the information.

Physical Models/Mental Models

A Story to Tell

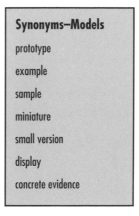

In a professional development conference in Holland, the program included scientists from a nearby brain research center and educators from around the world. It was a planned opportunity for the two camps to dialogue about the brain and learning. As the day unfolded, the scientists often showed various examples of the human brain. Some of them were of real brains in jars of formaldehyde, others were plastic models of various views or particular parts of the human brain, emphasizing one area of study.

As the collection of models grew, the tables were soon covered with these artifacts. It was obvious by the clusters of teachers around the tables at the break times that every adult in the room wanted to touch, handle, feel, and examine the models of the brain. The models were so compelling, it was difficult to stop the explorations and get back to the talks—a vivid testimony to the power of physical models in the teaching/learning scenario.

Things You Need You to Know

What's It All About?

Models are miniature prototypes that depict the real thing by representing it in a concrete way. Rather than a simple drawing, the model offers a three-dimensional look that often is to scale.

Joyce and Showers (1995) discuss five elements to sound staff development training for teachers: theory, demonstration, practice, feedback, and coaching. Inherent in the demonstration element is the idea of a model to illustrate and clarify. Although Joyce and Showers do not use exactly the same meaning of models as used in this book, it is a near cousin. Models illuminate and provide concrete evidence of the idea or topic under study.

For the sake of this discussion, models include plastic and rubber-molded models, bodily/kinesthetic and physically manipulable models, and models in the mind's eye.

Molded models offer a finished product for students to view and handle physically as they begin to organize the ideas in their minds. Bodily kinesthetic models invite students to "become" the thing (the letter A, the electrons and the protons, the exclamation point), or to construct a model on their own (the pulley; a Rube Goldberg invention). Mental models are the images created from the physical models. These mental models stay with the learner and provide clues for deep understanding. After students have touched a molded brain and created the parts of the brain with their bodies, they have a mental picture of a brain that serves them as they read and learn.

Models are like pets.

Models are like pets: both need to be touched; both become more familiar with handling; and both form indelible pictures in our minds even when they are not there.

Why Bother?

The implications for this best practice of nonlinguistic representations are directly linked to providing concrete the examples—the more concrete examples, the clearer the ideas become for the learner. When students create models for their learning, their understanding deepens. The implication of this best practice is to encourage teachers to incorporate models in the classroom as often as is practical.

> **When students create models for their learning, their understanding deepens.**

A Tiny Transfer to Try

Body Sculpture

This exercise concerns experiencing the power of physical models created through the bodily kinesthetic intelligence. Use small cooperative groups. Ask participants to use their bodily intelligence as they take turns pretending to become the parts of a plant, a well-developed paragraph, the World Wide Web, three branches of government, or a plant in the process of photosynthesis. Encourage participants to dialogue about how to use models for the content and subject areas they teach.

Family of Strategies: Cooperative Learning (6CL)

Strategy

Cooperative Learning

6CL

Cooperative Learning

A Story to Tell

David Johnson explains in his quiet, professorial way, "Cooperative learning is about kids caring as much about the other kids' success as they care about their own. It's more than a learning strategy. It's a way of life. And it's part of the mission of schooling to teach kids the social skills of collaboration and constructive controversy."

The words struck a chord that day that still resonates even today. After opening with that comment,

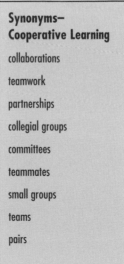

**Synonyms—
Cooperative Learning**

collaborations

teamwork

partnerships

collegial groups

committees

teammates

small groups

teams

pairs

Johnson modeled his beliefs during a week-long training of trainers. This is what happened.

There was a team in this training that tried the soul of a saint. The members were in constant conflict, bickering, arguing, and making very little progress on the various tasks presented. Johnson was continually stopping by the group, talking with them, facilitating a next step, and encouraging them to carry on and complete the given task.

When asked, in a private conversation, why he had not just given up on this team, David replied, "This is the group that needs me the most. They're the ones that need my help with social skills: communication, leadership, teamwork, and, yes, conflict resolution."

Things You Need You to Know

What's It All About?

Cooperative learning as a phrase signals several things: a collaboration of sorts, shared responsibility, a certain level of cooperation and trust; and, of course, a common goal.

Johnson, Johnson, and Holubec's (1986) classic, *Circles of Learning*, sets the conceptual model that includes positive interdependence, individual accountability, group processing, social skills, and face-to-face interaction (P-I-G-S-Face is the acronym that helps capture the five elements). In addition, Lev Vygotsky (1978) writes that first we learn through our verbalizations in a social setting and then, we internalize the ideas more clearly. This process makes a case for cooperative structures, which are like a centipede: both have multiple parts, both are a segmented whole, and both are most efficient when all the parts work in concert. The cooperative classroom has been described as a "bottoms-up classroom," because when kids are working in cooperative groups, they often lean over the table into the group and have their bottoms up in the air.

> **Cooperative structures...are like a centipede.**

Although the actual makeup of cooperative groups depends on a number of things, teachers make standard decisions in forming the groups: size, composition, task, roles, social skills, accountability, and reflection.

Size. The ideal size for some experts (Johnson, Johnson, & Holubec, 1986) is 2 to 3 members in a group, whereas for others (Kagan, 1989), the ideal number is 4 because the teacher can split them easily into a "pair of pairs."

Composition. Heterogeneous groups, mixing gender, race, ability , language, talent and challenges are preferred.

Task. The task varies with the teacher and the topic from textbook jigsaws to group work samples on large poster paper to more comprehensive projects.

Roles. Although the actual roles for a group depend on the task, there are generic roles that are frequently used:

        Materials Manager: Gets the stuff.

        Recorder: Power of the pen.

        Reporter: Speaker for the group.

        Encourager: Cheers team on to victory.

        Traveler: Scouts out ideas from other teams.

Social Skills. Social skills (encouraging, agreeing and sharing) must be explicitly targeted and taught as a part of the cooperative learning experiences.

Accountability. Part of the task assignment includes the expectations for the final product and/or for the steps and processes required.

Reflection. A structured reflection on the teamwork might be a Plus, Minus, Interesting (PMI), or reflective questions about what went well and what the team might do differently next time.

There are three kinds of interaction structures that follow the tenets of cooperative learning. These are whole group, small group, and partners. Figure 6.1 shows the three with examples of appropriate cooperative activities for the chosen group.

Whole Group
People Search   Human Graph   2-4-8

Small Group
Trios   Fours

Partners
Turn to your   Think/Pair/Share
partner and…

Figure 6.1 Cooperative group interaction structures.

Why Bother?

Cooperative learning is cited with this recommendation: "Of all the classroom strategies, cooperative learning may be the most flexible and powerful" (Marzano, Pickering, &

Pollock, 2001, p. 91). The authors are writing in their study of classroom instruction that works and are alluding to the quality of cooperative learning as a strategy that combines easily with other strategies. The obvious implication points to frequent and varied use of this strategy.

> **The authors are alluding to the quality of cooperative learning as a strategy that combines easily with other strategies.**

A Tiny Transfer to Try

Competent or Not?

Use groups of 4 or a "pair of pairs." Assign roles: starting with the tallest person and moving around the group counter-clockwise, select a materials manager, recorder, roving reporter, and encourager. Ask groups to define these four concepts on sections of a large sheet of poster paper folded in quarters:

> Unconscious Incompetence,
>
> Conscious Incompetence,
>
> Conscious Competence,
>
> Unconscious Competent.

Ask participants to unpack the ideas represented in each of the phases. As part of their work, they need to demonstrate the use of at least three multiple intelligences when they present their understandings to another small group. Set a time for the sharing.

Family of Strategies: Setting Objectives and Providing Feedback (7OF)

Strategies

7OF

Setting Objectives

Providing Feedback

 **Setting Objectives**

A Story to Tell

A veteran teacher explained, "The best teaching I ever did ended because the goals were not formally articulated, even though our results were extremely positive."

In an excited voice, speaking at a rapid rate, she went on, "Kid's Incorporated or KINC, was a multiage classroom of 8-to-12-year-old students. There were two teachers in a double room with a folding wall. Students and parents chose the alternative program. We were part of what was known as

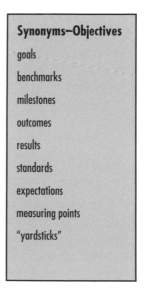

Synonyms–Objectives

goals

benchmarks

milestones

outcomes

results

standards

expectations

measuring points

"yardsticks"

the "open classroom" concept, and our kids were exposed to a rich and robust curriculum that involved skill groups in mathematics and reading, science experiments, and social studies projects. We went to an outdoor education camp every fall, with parents teaching the various offerings. The kids thrived in this setting and learning was happening at every level."

The listener asked the obvious questions, "What happened? Why did it fail if there were such positive outcomes?"

Speaking deliberately, she explained, "There were no standards frameworks at that time. Each teacher, or team of teachers in this case, designed the curriculum and instruction on his or her own. There were occasional articulation sessions between grade levels or departments, but basically, each level worked pretty discretely from any other. The experiences orchestrated for the students in KINC were of the highest quality. But the fatal flaw with the open classroom concept was the lack of documentation of curriculum goals and lack of formal accountability to assure that the goals were met. That would not happen today with the standards front and center in every school curriculum."

Things You Need You to Know

What's It All About?

Goals are like roadmaps.

Setting objectives is goal setting. It involves achieving certain accomplishments within a predetermined period of time. Goals are like roadmaps: both guide the journey. They provide the inspiration to begin the journey and the motivation to keep going. To be goal-driven is epitomized by the roadmap metaphor because travelers often pick a destination point for the day's trip and do not waver until they have made their goal. Goal-driven people are productive people because they know where they are going.

There are short-term goals that become an integral part of the classroom as students practice setting daily goals in various subjects for the required work or homework. In addition, there are long-term goals that require a number of steps along the way, as exemplified in comprehensive projects and performances.

Goals are part of the American culture, both in personal endeavors, in the corporate world, and in the realm of schooling. They are manifested in New Year's resolutions, self-help programs, corporate policy, and classroom interactions.

In a typical classroom scenario, teachers assign a project with a due date, and then help students work backward through the different phases of the process. It might sound like this: paper due date, back up to first draft due date, then back up to outline due date, notes due date, research-needed-by date, and finally, back to choosing the topic focus by a due date. Just as an aside, "backward mapping" is a term used fairly frequently in a standards-based model. It is a process that students must be familiar with and able to execute skillfully if they are to be successful.

Yet, goals can be elusive and goal setting can be evasive. There's a saying that comes to mind about the concept of goals and objectives. It queries, "If you don't know where you're going, how will you know when you get there?" Of course, there is wisdom in its simplicity.

■ ☐ ■ ☐ ■

Why Bother?

Implications for schooling are many and far-reaching. It is the American dream: the student goes off to college, prepares for a great career, lands the job of his or her dreams, marries, has children, and lives happily ever after. Although this fantasy probably has many flaws under close scrutiny, a number of the elements do become real goals of pursuit by young people.

Without doubt, the reigning method of setting learning objectives is found in the standards movement. Creating robust, rigorous, and rich standards for student learning with intermittent and measurable benchmarks serves as a viable model for setting objectives for student achievement.

> **Without doubt, the reigning method of setting learning objectives is found in the standards movement.**

For example, each content area has its basic set of concepts, skills, and procedures. By acknowledging the goal that all students will know and be able to do investigations in life science, the science objectives are clear to all.

A Tiny Transfer to Try

Design with the End in Mind: As Easy as One! Two! Three!

Divide the participants into grade-level, department, or interdisciplinary teams of about 3 to 4 people. Assign the five roles: materials manager, recorder, reporter, encourager, and traveler. Have three large sheets of poster paper and a set of fat markers on each table. Follow the three-step program outlined here.

One! Goals (Standards)

Ask grade level or department teams of teachers to use the generic set of standards in Figure 7.1 to select a robust content standard to use as their *target standard* or goal for the unit. Then, ask them to add several *additional process standards* that can be addressed easily as this unit of study unfolds. Have the recorder write these on large poster paper.

One! Standards/Goals

Target standards for the unit of study.

Subject(s): Language Arts (integrated with history, fine arts, and technology)

Unit: Speech/Debate

Content Standards Cluster: (required curricular content area(s))

History: Knowledge of continuity and change in the history of the United States and the world.

Use of tools of social science technology.

Language Arts: Participation in formal and informal presentations and discussions of issues and ideas.

Knowledge and proficiency in reading and evaluating nonfiction works and materials (biographies, newspapers, technical manuals).

Fine Arts: Knowledge of interrelationships of visual and performing arts to other disciplines.

Process Standards Cluster: (universal life skills)

1. Knowledge of processes and techniques for the production and exhibition of visual or performed arts.

2. Use of technological tools and other resources to locate, select, and organize information.

3. Examine problems and proposed solutions from multiple perspectives.

4. Develop and apply strategies based on one's own experience in preventing and solving problems.

5. Identify problems and their scope and elements.

Figure 7.1 Content and process standards clusters.

Two! Evidence (Performance)

Now, have the teams create a performance task for the students using a two-part model as shown in Figure 7.2: 1. You are and 2. You will...

Part 1 (You are . . .) sets up a stakeholder role for the students: "You are the Confederate general in the Civil War. Your troops are hungry and cold and wounded. The Yankees are advancing steadily. What will you do?"

Part 2 (You will . . .) sets up the requirements for the students: "You will need to include a map of the area, a letter for the messenger, a timeline of the events and a historical synopsis of the period."

Figure 7.2 Performance task.

Reflect on the richness of the performance task and the layering of the standards.

Three! Judgment (Rubric)

(Note: Step 3 is included in this exercise only to illustrate the complete cycle of setting objectives and providing feedback. Participants actually do this step after the discussion of Feedback in the next section of the book.)

After the teams have outlined the requirements, they must develop a scoring rubric for each of the required performances. In this case, they need a rubric for the map, the letter, the timeline, and the historical synopsis. Figure 7.3 shows a layout for a rubric for the map that needs to be developed.

Scoring Rubric: Civil War Map				
	Developing	Competent	Proficient	Expert
Accuracy				
Detail				
Key				

Figure 7.3 Scoring rubric: Civil War map.

70F ✓ Providing Feedback

A Story to Tell

While helping a customer who was trying to decide what to give a friend as a going away gift, the saleswoman shared the story of her son's gift to her of a heart monitor. "My son, Tom, had given his dad a heart monitor for Christmas because his dad is a marathon runner and Tom thought it would be the perfect gift. And it was."

Then, she continued, "On my birthday, he gave me a heart monitor. Of course, I thanked him warmly, but I wasn't that sure that I really wanted a heart monitor. I am just not that data/technology oriented. But to honor my son's thoughtfulness, I had my husband calibrate my new heart monitor, and I used it when I went for my morning walk."

With a huge-smile on her face, she shared her enthusiasm, "You will never know how much I love my heart monitor. It gives me instant and on-going feedback on my level of exertion. I know immediately if I am in the "zone" and if I am getting the most benefit from what I am doing. It signals me that I need to create more energy and I adjust accordingly. I can walk faster, move my arms, or increase my stride and watch the heart monitor for the effects of the improvement strategies."

> **Synonyms—Feedback**
>
> data
>
> input
>
> reflections
>
> comments
>
> evaluations
>
> critiques
>
> analyses

And, with that, the customer smiled, "Thank you for a great idea. I know just what to get her. She is an exercise nut, so this will be perfect."

Things You Need You to Know

What's It All About?

Feedback comprises all the things (comments, smiles, nods of acknowledgment, written signals) that provide guideposts to one's progress toward a stated (or unstated) goal. Feedback is data that are accessible, immediate, specific, relevant, and available. It is the reflection in the mirror that offers guidance and encouragement.
Feedback can be informal, deliberate comments from the coach in the field, or it can be more formal, encompassing achievement or production data that drive future decisions. Either way, feedback is a signal during the process of how things are going.

Joyce and Showers (1995) emphasize the importance of feedback in the coaching model for professional development. Checkups are the feedback that keeps things on track and authentic and allows change to occur in the adult learner. Feedback for younger learners is similar because it also provides needed checkpoints to learning.

Feedback is like a box of Wheaties (the "breakfast of champions"): both symbolize a peak performance, both fuel the process, both are catalysts to growth and change, and both feed the hunger of a potential winner.

Feedback is like a box of Wheaties.

In school settings, feedback can be through verbal communications and periodic written communications, and also through a more formal route called a scoring rubric, which is a particularly powerful method. For example, as students create portfolios of work, a predetermined rubric informs students that feedback (and judgments) will be given in the areas of *appearance*, *content*, and *reflective thinking* (Figure 7.4), established as criteria for success. Knowing the criteria (and the fully described indicators for each criterion) students are poised for relevant feedback on their final portfolio product. Scoring rubrics can be created by the teacher alone, or better yet, they can be developed collaboratively with students. In this way, students are clear and well informed of the criteria being used to evaluate their work.

	Not Evident	Complete	Notable	Exemplary
Appearance				
Content				
Reflections				

Figure 7.4 Rubric: student portfolios.

Why Bother?

> **The beauty of feedback is that it gives learners a chance to change for the better.**

Providing timely, specific, and relevant feedback on how well the process is going complements the strategy of setting objectives. The beauty of feedback is that it gives learners a chance to change for the better if what they are doing is not taking them in the right direction. Remember, as the ancient proverb sometimes attributed to Homer says, "There is many a slip 'twixt the cup and the lip." Feedback gives students the ammunition to be flexible in carrying out their plan to meet the objective.

A Tiny Transfer to Try

Criterion-Referenced Scoring Rubric

Keep the same departmental, grade-level, or interdisciplinary groups used in the previous Tiny Transfer *(Design with the End in Mind: As Easy as One! Two! Three!)* for this final step. Participants now advance to Step Three and complete the setting-objectives-and-feedback cycle started in that exercise by completing a scoring rubric. Use the instructions in that exercise to do this. See Figure 7.3 Scoring Rubric. After the chart is completed, have teams share ideas with each other. Discuss the role of feedback in the standards based classroom. Use Figure 7.5 to collect the ideas teams generate.

Feedback Methods	
Formal Feedback	Informal Feedback

Figure 7.5 Feedback methods.

Family of Strategies: Generating and Testing Hypotheses (8GH)

Strategy

Generating and Testing Hypotheses

8GH

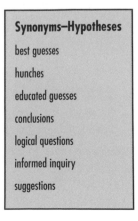

8GH

Generating and Testing Hypotheses

A Story to Tell

A fifth grade teacher asks his class to think about the dinosaurs. "Asteroids hit the earth and blow dust that blocks out the sun, the ferns die, there are no plants, and there is a disruption of the food chain. That is one *theory* about why the dinosaurs became extinct. I want you to come up with your best thinking on this. Why did the dinosaurs become extinct?"

After some time working in pairs, one boy stands up, "It's just a *theory*, but we think the dinosaurs

Synonyms–Hypotheses
best guesses
hunches
educated guesses
conclusions
logical questions
informed inquiry
suggestions

■ □ ■ □ ■

froze to death. We believe they drifted into the Arctic and were not able to survive in the frigid climate. Eventually, they all died."

Another group reporter say, "It's just a *theory* but we hypothesize that the dinosaurs died off because they ate plants that were infected with poisonous bugs. The plant eaters ate the plants with the insects on them and, then, the meat eaters ate the plant eaters and also became sick. The only thing that survived were the plants that man used for food later."

Things You Need You to Know

What's It All About?

Hypothesizing and theory making is an integral process of the human brain. The innate curiosity and inquisitiveness of human beings lead to predictions, hypotheses, and possible explanations for the phenomenon being observed. This "best practice" of having students generate and test hypotheses is integral to the problem-solving/decision-making process. After facts are gathered, the human mind automatically tries to make sense of the information. That effort to make meaning—to synthesize—causes the mind to search for relevant patterns, related ideas, and meaningful connections. That is how insights occur and logical theories begin to emerge. Testing hypotheses is proving that the hunch, insight, or theory was correct.

A hypothesis focuses the question for the investigation. It suggests a possible explanation for something that is occurring. This generating and testing hypotheses process occurs repeatedly in everyday situations as people ponder these kinds of situations: Why is this plant dying? What is the fastest route? How can I motivate her? What is that noise in the car? Where is that smell coming from? Why did the dessert flop like that? What happens when I arrange the furniture this way? Generating hypotheses is like riding a bike: both require skillful handling, both depend on a balanced position, both can have disastrous results when carelessness prevails, and both are complex processes that require courage on the part of the learner.

Generating hypotheses is like riding a bike.

Gopnik, Meltzoff, and Kuhl (1999) note in their book, *Scientists in the Crib*, that even infants exhibit the skills of generating and testing their hypotheses. Who has not observed the trial-and-error process of babies who try over and over and over again to grasp an object?

A folksy example demonstrates how natural the process of generating and testing hypotheses is to the human brain. A family member observes that the freezer in the refrigerator has formed so much ice during the past few days that the door won't close tightly. She mentions it to her husband, and he wonders if it is related to the leaking water that just drips and collects in one spot. He goes on to theorize that the refrigerator and freezer doors might need new seal casings Then, he continues to hypothesize that if the seal is tighter, less air gets in, thus, less chance for ice to form and, if no dripping water, no ice. Of course, testing this hypothesis leads to installing new seal casings and observing the results.

Another example from the classroom shows young students working with magnets. They begin to formulate ideas about what "sticks" and what "doesn't stick" to the magnets. Of course, following the natural course of events, after students have developed a theory about magnets and magnetic fields, they must "test" their theory with examples and non-examples. Through trial and error, they can refine this theory and write more credible hypotheses.

Why Bother?

Students must become skilled thinkers, productive problem solvers, and mindful decision makers if they are to thrive in the world they will inherit.

Students must become skilled thinkers, productive problem solvers, and mindful decision makers if they are to thrive in the world they will inherit. Generating and testing hypotheses is an inherent skill in these sophisticated processes. Being skillful with the scientific method in problem solving, decision making, and investigating benefits students as they learn the micro skills of higher order thinking: visualizing, hypothesizing, predicting, analyzing, understanding cause and effect, comparing and contrasting, and theorizing.

A Tiny Transfer to Try

Knowing What to Do

"Knowing what to do when you don't know what to do" is how Piaget defined intelligent behavior. Teachers can keep students engaged with problems, puzzles, and riddles by using open-ended and somewhat ambiguous examples. These require the mind to consider several courses of action, thus exercising the mind and keeping the learner more intently engaged. In fact, the most promising kinds of exercises are the ones that don't present one right answer.

Organize participants into cooperative teams. Explain that they are going to work with an inquiry model called problem-based learning (PBL). Each team will address the problem and come up with a solution. There are innumerable ways to approach the problem.

The Problem

You are a member of the Board of Directors for an office complex in which the construction process has just been completed. The cranes are gone and, in fact, all tenants are moved in. You and the other board members are pleased that the building is at full capacity. However, some tenants have surfaced a concern and several have threatened to break their leases. The problem they describe is about the slow elevators. They claim that their employees are upset and disgruntled because they have to wait so long at the elevators. The board is meeting to discuss the situation that has surfaced. What will you recommend?

The Process

1. Use a Fishbone graphic to analyze the problem (see Figure 5.5 for an example form).

2. Brainstorm possible alternatives.

3. Advocate a particular solution, stating your hypothesis to justify your choice.

4. Present the solution to the other groups. Convince them of its merit.

Share ideas about how to use hypothesizing in the classroom for inquiry and problem solving.

■□■□■

Family of Strategies: Questions and Cues and Advanced Organizers (9QCA)

Strategies

Questions and Cues

Advanced Organizers

Questions and Cues

A Story to Tell

A seasoned consultant tells a story about his student teaching days, and how he inadvertently learned about good questioning techniques. "Her name was Mimi Potter," he says and goes on, "she was my critic teacher when I was doing practice teaching in Champagne-Urbana, IL."

Synonyms—Cues
prompts
hints
clues
previews
scans
glimpses

He explains, "Before teaching a lesson, Mrs. Potter would sit down with me to talk about the day's plans. After a time, I realized she was asking four questions each time: 'What are you planning to do? What do you think will go well? What might you have to do differently? Do you need any help from me?'"

He continues, "Interestingly, after the day, we would sit down and she would go through those same four questions with a slight shift in tenses: 'What were you planning to do? What do you think went well? What might you do differently? Do you need any help from me?' The questions left an indelible mark on me."

"I was a beginning English teacher at New Trier High School, in Winnetka, IL," he explained and continued "I found myself asking *Mrs. Potter's Questions* to help my students plan and reflect on their work. In fact, I would ask the same set of four questions and get such good results, that I started sharing the idea with other teachers."

Things You Need You to Know

What's It All About?

Questions are inquiries that prompt thinking and facilitate the process of problem solving or decision making.

Questions and cues are like the yellow warning light on the traffic signal.

Questions are cueing techniques that act as a catalyst to deeper or more complex thinking. Questions and cues are like the yellow warning light on the traffic signal: both alert the mind to incoming signals, both are part of a continuous system of signals, and both serve as reminders that bring the mind to a more ready state.

From the time Bloom and his colleagues (1956) published the infamous Bloom's Taxonomy, students have been bombarded with questions at the six various levels ranging from knowledge and comprehension to application, analysis, synthesis, and evaluation. Students have been asked to list, recall, use, dissect, create, and judge topics of the moment, across content areas.

Questions that cue "prime the pump" by setting the stage for further investigation by the learner or by foreshadowing the reading that is about to happen. In textbooks, cueing questions are questions in bold-face type: **What are three kinds of rocks?** or **What were the causes of WWII?** Or, they may be more specific questions to cue the learner to look for the answer: *Where did Lewis and Clark journey?* or *How did the slaves escape to the North?*

To focus for a moment on cues as opposed to questions that cue, there are subtle and not so subtle hints that help student anticipate what is about to come in the reading or in the discussion. These are "text organizers" that signal the reader or listener in narratives about what to anticipate. For example:

1. "First," "next," and "finally" cue the reader to a sequence of steps.

2. "There are seven ..." cues the reader or listener that there are seven ideas to anticipate.

3. "In the beginning," "during" and "at the end" cue a chronology of events.

4. "To compare" and "by contrast" cue the reader or listener to note similarities and differences.

All of these serve to alert the reader. They help to create a mind ready to receive input in an informed way; that is, in a way that makes it easier for the mind to capture the information through logical connections.

One of the most powerful questions to activate prior knowledge and to foster making connections in the mind is captured in what are called Mr. Parnes' Questions (See Figure 9.1).

Mr. Parnes' Questions

1. How does this connect with something I already know?

2. How might I use this in the future?

Figure 9.1 Mr. Parnes' questions.

The first of the two questions focuses on prior knowledge. But, the second question begs for relevant applications that may also reference past experiences. To illustrate how skillful teachers use questions and cues to activate prior knowledge, there is a set of questions called Mr. Pete's Pointers (Figure 9.2).

Mr. Pete's Pointers

1. Would you tell me more about that?

2. What else?

3 Can you give me a specific example?

Figure 9.2: Mr. Pete's pointers.

These three "probes" help teachers encourage students to elaborate on their responses or let them give other students opportunities to add to the idea or to generate another idea. The first one, "Would you tell me more about that?" prompts students to go into more depth and to elaborate on the original, which is often a one-word response. The second question, "What else?" is posed as the teacher looks around the entire classroom. With this question, the teacher is looking for multiple answers to the original questions. The third question, "What else can someone say about this idea?" cues students to illustrate an abstract idea by giving a more concrete specific example to illustrate its meaning. This third question requires students to connect personally to the topic under discussion.

Why Bother?

The implications of this "best practice" of *questions* and *cues* focuses on the constructivist idea of "activating prior knowledge" in the K-12 classroom. In theory, questions and cues activate background experiences and what the learner already knows about the topic.

A simple diagram in Figure 9.3 explains this theory of prior knowledge.

Traditional Methods	Constructivist Approach
Pre-Learning Strategies	PRE-LEARNING STRATEGIES
During the Learning Strategies	During the Learning Strategies
POST-LEARNING STRATEGIES	Post-Learning Strategies

Figure 9.3: Prior knowledge.

In traditional classrooms, teachers have emphasized three types of strategies used sequentially: *pre*-learning strategies to set up the learning; questions or prompts *during* the lesson, and *post*-learning activities to ensure that the learning occurred. The emphasis is usually on

> **The more the mind can focus on the topic, the more fertile the mind will be in making connections.**

post-learning strategies. In the constructivist model, the theory holds that the learner constructs meaning in the mind by making neural connections. Based on this belief, the more the mind can focus on the topic, the more fertile the mind will be making connections. Thus, the emphasis in on *pre*-learning strategies.

A Tiny Transfer to Try

Mrs. Poindexter's Questions

Introduce two cueing questions that help students anticipate solutions in their problem solving:

1. Where are you stuck?

2. How will you get unstuck?

Explain that these two cues move the learner along in his or her thinking. The analysis involved in answering the first question may help point out certain key things that may be critical to any substantial progress. The second question moves the learner into a proactive state of mind, fostering movement forward.

Then, give the participants a puzzling challenge: How many times between noon and midnight does the minute hand pass the hour hand?

Use A-B pairs to do the problem solving, and ask pairs to use Mrs. Poindexter's Questions to analyze their process.

Discuss "getting stuck" and "how they got unstuck." Then talk about the value of this to students and ways to introduce it in class.

9QCA

Ⓠ Advance Organizers

A Story to Tell

As soon as someone says, "I have a story to tell you ...," our ears perk up, and we are poised to listen to what comes next. In fact, a speaker once told this story. "I always begin my talk with this line, 'As I understand it, it's my job to talk and it's your job to listen. If you finish before I do, let me know'." After the laughter dies down, I continue, "Today, I want to talk about three salient points. The first is...blah, blah, blah. The second point is...blah, blah, blah, and I never get to the third...it keeps them anticipating that third point and they just keep listening."

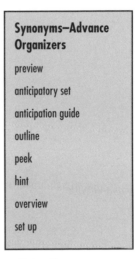

Synonyms–Advance Organizers

preview

anticipatory set

anticipation guide

outline

peek

hint

overview

set up

Although the activity in the speaker's story may seem like a mean thing to do, it illustrates the power of advance organizers. The three-points idea sets up the anticipation to listen for three things. The learner is ready to capture the three things and, in fact, is frustrated when the "third" thing never comes.

Things You Need You to Know

What's it All About?

The advance organizer is a cueing device that provides a look at what is coming. It is the preview or the glimpse of the full piece. Advance organizers may be questions and cues as discussed earlier, but they may also take the form of graphic organizers, discussed as non-linguistic representations.

Ausubel (1978) is credited with the research that supports advance organizers, such as the structured overview, as pre-learning tools in the constructivist classroom. Robinson (1970) supports the theory with the pre-learning tool called SQ3R: Survey, Question, Read, Recite, Review.

To know the power of advanced organizers is to understand a syllabus, a table of contents, a chart, or diagram. These structures provide a preview, an advanced look at what is about to come. These advanced organizers provide a mind set for incoming information. They activate prior knowledge and set up patterns in the mind to use in connecting new information.

An advance organizer is like a movie trailer.

An advance organizer is like a movie trailer: both provide a peek preview of what is to come, both tend to focus on the highlights, and both leave the viewer wanting more. Advance organizers are teasers that serve to entice the participant into continuing to search for more information. They want to know what happens next.

When, in working with mediated journals, the teacher labels the pages of the journal for students to use, he or she is, in essence, providing an "advance look" at the notes that will fill those pages. Advance organizers can be simple text organizers (Now..., then..., and next...) as described in the cueing discussion earlier; they can be delineated procedures (SQ3R) that guide the learning; or they can be graphic tools or maps (webs) that point the way for student learning.

Why Bother?

The strongest implication of advance organizers for classroom practice lies in the very fact that advance organizers do just what they say— they organize in advance of the reading or learning. For example, teachers may ask students to scan a chapter and create a web of ideas about what they predict may be in the reading. This web then can serve as an organizer that students can add to as they continue to read. It can also serve as a tool for planning their writing.

> **Advance organizers do just what they say—they organize in advance of the reading or learning.**

A Tiny Transfer to Try

Skim/Scan Scam

Tell the story of the nun who was discouraged with her progress in a speed-reading course:

Every week the members of the class would report their times as they practiced "speed-reading" techniques, but the nun showed no improvement. The instructor asked her to explain exactly what she was doing when she read. The nun described a typical reading process and said something about "reading every word." With that, the instructor reminded the nun not to read every word, but to skim and scan the text for important information; to read rapidly, and get the gist of what was going on. The nun nodded, and then class continued.

The next week, the nun had astonishing results on her speed exercises. The instructor asked what had happened, what had made the difference. She replied, "I'm used to following the rules, when you gave me permission *not to read every word*, it was easy to speed up my reading."

Ask participants to skim and scan a text entry "Text for Skimming" (see Figure 9.4) and jot down key ideas using a graphic organizer of choice. Then, ask them to read it more thoroughly and check their notes to see if they caught the gist of the text.

Discuss applications of teaching skimming and scanning skills to students. Decide how to introduce these skills and how to provide lots of practice with them at the various grade levels.

Excerpt of "The 12th Bracey Report on the Condition of Public Education" by G. Bracey in *Phi Delta Kappan*, 2002, 84(2), 135–137. Reprinted with permission.

For comic relief, let us now turn to a story that the *New York Times* ran under the headline "The Elderly Man and the Sea?" In New York, a Brooklyn mother with a master's degree in English, Jeanne Heifetz, noticed that a New York Regents test had modified a passage from a book. At first, she thought it was just a glitch of some kind. Then she saw another passage that was altered even more. Two accidents? Heifetz didn't think so, and she was right.

(continued)

Figure 9.4 Text for skimming.

It turns out that the New York Department of Education has "sensitivity review guidelines" to ensure that no child feels uncomfortable taking the test—as if the test's importance didn't already guarantee butterflies (recall that the SAT 9 now comes with instructions on what to do if a child vomits on the answer sheet). What sort of alterations did Heifetz notice? All mentions of Judaism were removed from excerpts of Isaac Bashevis Singer, and the sentence "Jews are Jews and Gentiles are Gentiles" was entirely deleted from an excerpt from *An American Childhood*, by Annie Dillard.

Indeed, few things seemed too trivial for New York's sensitivity police. "Skinny" became "thin," "fat" became "heavy," "gringo lady" became "American lady," fine California wine and seafood" became "fine California seafood," and on and on. In a passage dealing with Frank Conroy's memoir, *Stop-Time*, "hell" turned into "heck," and the censors excised all references to sex, religion, nudity, and potential violence (in the form of two boys about to kill a snake).

Naturally, Heifetz's discovery offended many people, including the authors of the bowdlerized texts, many of whom she took the trouble to contact. The National Coalition Against Censorship, the Association of American Publishers, the New York Civil Liberties Union, and PEN (Poets, Playwrights, Editors, Essayists, and Novelist) sent a joint letter of protest to Richard Mills, the state education commissioner.

Roseanne DeFabio, one of Mills' assistant commissioners, uttered a statement that became an instant classic: "Even the most wonderful writers don't write literature for children to take on a test."[2] Exactly.

Within two days, Mills had left DeFabio twisting in the wind, declaring that the altering of texts would be terminated. That announcement came after the practice was zapped by Diane Ravitch in the *New York Times*[3], Anna Quindlen in *Newsweek*[4], Margo Adler of "All Things Considered," and the editors of the *Washington Times*[5]. Quindlen, who had suffered similar editing from ETS, observed that *The Catcher in the Rye, To Kill a Mockingbird,* and *The Merchant of Venice* would all fail to meet the standards of the Regents exam. "Here is the most shocking question among the New York state guidelines," Quindlen wrote. "'Does the material assume values not shared by all test takers?' There is no book worth reading, no poem worth writing, no essay worth analyzing that assumes the same values for all. That sentence is the death of intellectual engagement."

(continued)

Figure 9.4 (continued).

The critics voiced concern over the ethics and aesthetics of chopping passages. None pointed out that the sensitivity guidelines defeated their own purpose. The guidelines were intended to ensure that students taking the test did not become "uncomfortable." One can only imagine their discomfort when asked questions whose answers *depended* on the deleted passages. In *Learning All the Time*, John Holt discussed differences between the way the Suzuki method of violin instruction is applied in Japan and in the United States. Apparently perceiving that this discussion might offend *somebody*, the sensitivity monitors in New York deleted the passages from the excerpt on the test. Yet the students were asked questions about the differences. Even more egregious, in Chekhov's story "The Upheaval," a wealthy woman strip searches her servants in an effort to find a missing brooch. This passage was omitted. Then the students were asked to write an essay, based on the story, on the meaning of human dignity.

Figure 9.4 (continued).

Appendix A

PEOPLE SEARCH KEY: Best Practices That Make the Difference (Based on R. Marzano, J. Pollock and D. Pickering (2001), *Classroom Instruction that Works: Research-based strategies for increasing student achievement.* Copyright 2000. Reprinted by Permission of McREL).

1SD Similarities/Differences	2SN Summarizing/Note taking	3RR Reinforcing Effort/Recognition
Compares teaching for the test to learning for a lifetime.	Defends one summary statement: "Great Men make Great Events" or "Great Events make Great Men".	Argues for or against rewards, praise and recognition as student motivators.
4HP Homework/Practice	**5NR Non-linguistic Representations**	**6CL Cooperative Learning**
Completes the analogy... Homework : Practice :: ____ : ____	Explains the symbol (: and gives you a new one...	Ranks three elements of CL: __Roles __Social Skills __Task
7OF Objectives/Feedback	**8GH Generating and Testing Hypotheses**	**9QCA Questions, Cues, Advance Organizers**
Discusses the statement, "Feedback is the breakfast of champions."	Hypothesizes that, "If emotions drive attention and attention drives memory, then..."	Shares a memory cue such as HOMES for the names of the five Great Lakes...

■□■□■

PEOPLE SEARCH—On Your Own

(Based on *Classroom Instruction That Works* by Marzano, Pickering, and Pollock, 2001)

FIND SOMEONE WHO:

1SD Similarities/Differences	2SN Summarizing/Note taking	3RR Reinforcing Effort/Recognition
4HP Homework/Practice	5NR Non-linguistic Representation	6CL Cooperative Learning
7OF Objectives/Feedback	8GH Generating and Testing Hypotheses	9QCA Questions, Cues, Advance Organizers

BIBLIOGRAPHY

Ausubel, D. (1978). *Educational psychology: A cognitive view* (2nd ed.). New York: Holt, Rinehart, & Winston.

Bloom, B. S., Engelhart, M. S., Furst, E. J., Hill, W. H., & Kratwohl, D. R. (1956). *Taxonomy of educational objectives: Cognitive domain, Handbook 1.* New York: David McKay Co.

Bruer, J. (1999). *Myth of the first three years: A new understanding of early brain development and lifelong learning.* New York: The Free Press.

Burke, K., Fogarty, R., & Belgrade, S. (2001). *The portfolio connection* (2nd ed.). Thousand Oaks, CA: Corwin.

Caine, G., Caine, R. N., & Crowell, S. (1999). *Mindshifts: A brain-compatible process for professional development and the renewal of education* (2nd ed.). Tucson, AZ: Zephyr Press.

Caine, R. N., & Caine, G. (1991). *Making connections: Teaching and the human brain.* Alexandria, VA: Association for Supervision and Curriculum Development.

Caine, R. N., & Caine, G. (1994). *Making connections: Teaching and the human brain.* New York: Innovative Learning Publications: Addison-Wesley Publishing.

Cooney, W. C., Cross, B., & Trunk, B. (1993). *From Plato to Piaget: The greatest theorists from across the centuries and around the world.* New York: University Press of America.

D'Arcangelo, M. (2000). The scientist in the crib: A conversation with Andrew Meltzoff. *Educational Leadership, 58*(3), 8–13.

Deming, W. E. (1986). *Out of the crisis.* Cambridge, MA: The MIT Press.

Diamond, M., & Hobson, J. (1998). *Magic trees of the mind: How to nurture your child's intelligence, creativity, and healthy emotions from birth to adolescence.* New York: Dutton.

Eisner, E. (1979). *The educational imagination: On the design and evaluation of school programs.* New York: Macmillan Publishing.

Feuerstein, R. (1980). *Instrumental enrichment.* Baltimore: University Park Press.

Fogarty, R. (2001). *Differentiated learning: Different strokes for different folks.* Chicago: Fogarty & Associates.

Fogarty, R. (2001). *Student learning standards: A blessing in disguise.* Chicago: Fogarty & Associates.

Fogarty, R. (2001). *Teachers make the difference: A framework for quality.* Chicago: Fogarty & Associates.

Fogarty, R. (2002). *Brain compatible classrooms* (2nd ed.). Thousand Oaks, CA: Corwin.

Fogarty, R. (2002). *Making sense of the research on the brain and learning.* Chicago: Fogarty & Associates.

Goleman, D. (1995). *Emotional intelligence: Why it can matter more than IQ.* New York: Bantam Books.

Gardner, H. (1983). *Frames of mind: The theory of multiple intelligences.* New York: Basic Books.

Gardner, H. (1999). *Intelligence reframed: Multiple intelligences for the 21st century.* New York: Basic Books.

Gopnik, A., Meltzoff, A., & Kuhl, P. (1999). *The scientist in the crib: Minds, brains, and how children learn.* New York: William Morrow.

Hannaford, C. (1995). *Smart moves: Why learning is not all in your head.* Arlington, VA: Great Ocean Publishers.

Hart, L. (1983). *Human brain, human learning.* Kent, WA: Books for Educators.

Hyerle, D. (1996). *Visual tools for constructing knowledge.* Alexandria, VA: Association for Supervision and Curriculum Development.

Jensen, E. (1999). *Teaching with the brain in mind.* Alexandria, VA: Association for Supervision and Curriculum Development.

Jensen, E. (2000). *Brain-based learning: The new science of teaching and training* (revised ed.). Thousand Oaks, CA: Corwin.

Jensen, E. (2000). Moving with the brain in mind. *Educational Leadership 58*(3), 34–37.

Johnson, D. W., Johnson, R. T., & Holubec, E. J. (1986). *Circles of learning: Cooperation in the classroom.* Alexandria, VA: Association for Supervision and Curriculum Development.

Joyce, B. R., & Showers, B. (1983). *Power in staff development through research and training.* Alexandria, VA: Association for Supervision and Curriculum Development.

Joyce, B. R., & Showers, B. (1995). *Student achievement through staff development* (2d ed.). White Plains, NY: Longman.

Kagan, S. (1989). Cooperation works! *Educational Leadership, 47*(4), 12–15.

Kerman, S. (1979). Teacher expectations and student achievement. *Phi Delta Kappan 60*(10): 716–718.

Kohn, A. (1993). *Punished by rewards.* New York: Houghton Mifflin.

Kotulak, R. (1996). *Inside the brain: Revolutionary discoveries of how the mind works.* Kansas City, KS: Andrews and McMeel.

LeDoux, J. (1996). *The emotional brain: The mysterious underpinnings of emotional life.* New York: Simon and Schuster.

Lyman, F., & McTighe, J. (1988). Cueing thinking in the classroom: The promise of theory-embedded tools. *Educational Leadership, 45*(7), 18–24.

Marzano, R., Norford, J., Paynter, D., Pickering, D., & Gaddy, B. (2001). *A handbook for classroom instruction that works.* Alexandria, VA: Association for Supervision and Curriculum Development.

Marzano, R., Pickering, D., & Pollock, J. (2001). *Classroom instruction that works: Research-based strategies for increasing student achievement.* Alexandria , VA: Association for Supervision and Curriculum Development.

Miles, M., & Huberman, A. B. (1994). *Qualitative data analysis: A sourcebook of new methods* (2nd ed.). Thousand Oaks, CA: Sage.

Motivation and rewards [electronic booklet]. (2001). San Diego, CA: The Brain Store. Available from www.thebrainstore.com

Pete, B., & Fogarty, R. J. (2003). *Twelve brain principles that make the difference.* Thousand Oaks, CA: Corwin.

Piaget, J. (1954). *The construction of reality in the child.* New York: Basic Books.

Pinker, S. (1997). *How the mind works.* New York: W.W. Norton.

Pinker, S. (2002). *The blank slate: The modern denial of human nature.* New York: Viking.

Robinson, F. P. (1970). *Effective study.* New York: Harper & Row.

Rowe, M. B. (1974). Wait time and rewards as instructional variables, their influence on language, logic and fate control: Part 1. Wait-time. *Journal of Research in Science Teaching, 11,* 81–94.

Sousa, D. (2001). *How the brain learns* (2nd ed.). Thousand Oaks, CA: Corwin.

Sprenger, M. (1999). *Learning and memory: The brain in action.* Alexandria, VA: Association for Supervision and Curriculum Development.

Sylwester, R. (1995). *Celebration of neurons: An educator's guide to the human brain.* Alexandria, VA: Association for Supervision and Curriculum Development.

Sylwester, R. (1999). *Student brains, school issues: A collection of articles.* Thousand Oaks, CA: Corwin.

Sylwester, R. (2000). Unconscious emotions, conscious feelings. *Educational Leadership, 58*(3), 20–24.

Varlas, L. (2002). Getting acquainted with the essential nine. *ASCD Curriculum Update* (Winter), 4–5.

Vygotsky, L. (1978). *Mind in society.* Cambridge, MA: Harvard University Press.

Walberg, H. J. (1999). Productive teaching. In H. C. Waxman & H. J. Walberg (Eds.), *New directions for teaching practice and research* (pp. 75–104). Berkeley, CA: McCutchen Publishing.

Westwater, A., & Wolfe, P. (2000). The brain compatible curriculum. *Educational Leadership, 58*(3), 49–52.

Wolfe, P. (2000). *Brain matters.* Alexandria, VA: Association for Supervision and Curriculum Development.